SHIPPING
OF THE
RIVER FORTH

To Gordon and Jean Fettis
who both grew up and met
on the shores of the Forth

Shipbreaking has been an important industry on the River Forth since the dawn of steamships. From Alloa to Inverkeithing, some of the world's most famous ships have met their end. None is more famous than the first *Mauretania* of 1907, a Blue Riband holder for over twenty years and sister ship to the *Lusitania*. Here she is about to pass under the Forth Rail Bridge in 1935 on the way to Rosyth for scrapping.

SHIPPING
OF THE
RIVER FORTH

WILLIAM F. HENDRIE

TEMPUS

Anstruther is a popular seaside holiday town and its famous Fisheries Museum is a popular attraction, telling the story of the fishing industry from the time when the first written references occur in the chronicles of the monasteries in the thirteenth century. It was, however, not until the eighteenth century that fishing became a full-time occupation for many menfolk in the coastal villages along both sides of the Firth. The ending of the Napoleonic Wars in 1815 opened up European markets and gave the Scottish herring fishing industry a considerable boost. By the 1860s two-thirds of the Scottish catch was being exported to the Continent with the herring being sold as far away as Russia. By this time the Scottish fishermen and the fisher lassies who cured the catch followed the herring shoals right down the East Coast as far as the south of England providing them with months of regular work. Despite sailing further from their home ports, the fishing boats throughout this period remained small open-hulled undecked vessels as the fishermen insisted that this made it easier to handle the drift nets and the catches which they brought aboard. Although the first steam drifter was built in Aberdeen in 1868, the cost of such a vessel, meant most of the fishermen in the Forth still operated sailing boats right up until the end of the nineteenth century. The most popular design amongst the fishermen of the Forth ports was the 'Fifie', which was broad beamed and had straight stem and stern posts, with two sails. The largest were between 45-50ft long and by the beginning of the 1900s some of their owners installed paraffin-fueled engines to provide an auxiliary means of power and also extend their range. Scottish fishing enjoyed its most successful and prosperous year in 1913 when there were 30,000 men, manning almost 10,000 boats. The following year, however, the outbreak of the First World War ended all that as the fishermen made up the majority of the Royal Navy Reserve and were required for duty.

First published 2002
Copyright © William F. Hendrie, 2002

Tempus Publishing Limited
The Mill, Brimscombe Port,
Stroud, Gloucestershire, GL5 2QG
www.tempus-publishing.com

ISBN 0 7524 2117 4

TYPESETTING AND ORIGINATION BY
Tempus Publishing Limited
PRINTED IN GREAT BRITAIN BY
Midway Colour Print, Wiltshire

Contents

Acknowledgements

My thanks to all who have supplied photographs for this book, including Dr Arthur Down, Ronnie Rusack, Isabel McNab, William Johnston and Forth Ports plc. I am also indebted to my friend Guthrie Pollock and my editor at Tempus Publishing, Campbell McCutcheon, who both share my love of the Forth, for their time and patience in assisting with the layout of these pages.

Her Majesty The Queen's Yacht *Britannia* is now berthed in Leith. Built at John Brown's on the Clyde it is fitting that she is to spend her retirement in Scotland. Here she is sometime in the 1950s performing one of her official duties.

Introduction

The River Forth has for centuries been Scotland's most important link with the continent. As long ago as the days of the Romans, heavily laden galleys brought cargoes of both essentials and luxuries to Cramond to supply the troops who manned the outermost line of defence of their vast empire, Antonine's Wall, which stretched across the country's narrow waist from Bridgeness to Bowling on the Clyde. Later raven-prowed longboats ferried their Viking crews across the North Sea to raid and plunder the early coastal settlements along the Firth. As a lasting legacy they left behind traces of their language in the form of many place names; both Firth and Forth are derived from the same root as the Norwegian word fiord, meaning an inlet. There are eleven firths around the coast of mainland Scotland and a further ten in the Shetland Islands, but none has had such a major effect on the history and development of Scotland as the Forth.

It was from the Forth that the most famous of 'skeely' skippers, Sir Patrick Spence of ballad fame, set sail on his ill fated voyage to bring the Little Maid of Norway across the North Sea to be monarch of Scotland. Again it was in the Forth that the Scottish navy was born in the shape of the *Yellow Carvel* under the command of Sir Alexander Wood. Then, to ensure Scottish naval supremacy over the Auld Enemy the English, Scotland's first Royal Naval dockyard was established at Newhaven on the coast near Edinburgh to construct the *Great Michael*, which, as indicated by her proud title, was indeed the largest battleship of her age. Every oak tree in Fife except those in the royal hunting forest around Falkland Palace were felled to provide the longest straightest planks of wood for the hull of the *Great Michael* and once complete she was rowed all the way up river to Airth to be fitted out by the skilled craftsmen of that little inland port, a reminder indeed of how the waters of the Forth brought prosperity to places right into the heart of Central Scotland.

When comparatively more peaceful times arrived in the sixteenth century, the merchants of Alloa, Bo'ness and Culross and other ports along the Forth seized the opportunity to develop trade still further and established the Scottish staple at de Veere in the Netherlands centuries before the present much debated European Union was even a gleam in an ambitious politician's eye. Throughout the middle ages and beyond their small ships plied to and fro across the North Sea, or the German Ocean as it was then known, exporting heavy cargoes of coal and salt. Once these were sold the good profits made were used in turn to buy

Flemish linen and the luxury goods such as silks and spices imported by the ships of the Dutch East India Co. 'Guid gear gaes in sma' bulk' as the old Scottish saying goes and once safely stowed in the wooden kists in the captain's cabin in the stern these valuable items still left the ships' holds empty. Rather than sail home light or in ballast, the wily Scottish skippers therefore exploited this situation to make even more money by filling the space available with heavier cargoes such as iron, white and blue decorated Delft pottery tiles and rougher red pantiles ideal for roofing. Their colourful addition to Scottish domestic architect is indeed still visible in many coastal towns and villages along both shores of the Forth from Kincardine and Culross up river to Crail and Dunbar on opposite sides at the mouth of the Firth.

King James VI of Scotland and I of England referred to Fife as a beggar's mantle fringed with gold, emphasizing the importance of the Wee Kingdom's ports in helping to create the nation's wealth in the days when poor roads made it difficult if not impossible to transport heavy loads inland. Such was equally true of places on the Lothian shore with Bo'ness or to give it its full name, Borrowstounness, the Burgh Town On The Point, claiming to be the first place in Scotland where coal was exploited because it could be loaded immediately into ships for onward transportation. Following King James' accession to the English throne in 1603 on his only royal return visit to Scotland in 1617, the monarch went out of his way to visit the Moat Pit in Culross Bay, which was regarded as one of the wonders of the age as its careful siting by Sir George Bruce enabled the coal which it produced to be emptied directingly into the holds of waiting sailing ships to export it to the continent. Eight years later the Moat was disastrously flooded and destroyed as a result of the famous Great March Storm, which coincidentally, superstitiously marked the death of the king, as it swept and battered the coasts of the Forth, providing a stern reminder of the power of the weather.

Two hundred years later the coming of steam power in the nineteenth century permitted safer and more reliable regular commerce to be established with the introduction of famous Forth-based shipping companies including those of Currie, Gibson Rankine and Salvesen. To this day there are scheduled cargo services sailing every week between the Forth and Rotterdam and the other principal ports of Northern Europe while the giant oil tankers, which fill their tanks daily at Hound Point Oil Terminal boost still further the volume and value of this trade. The concentration of trade by the use of these vessels of up to 300,000 tons and the more rapid turn round made possible by the extensive use of box ships, may give the appearance that docks and harbours along the river are quieter nowadays but shipping on the Forth has in truth never been more important as the introduction of a new daily passenger and vehicle roll on/roll off ferry service from Rosyth to Zeebrugge in Belgium acts as a reminder. Its operator Superfast Ferries, a division of the Greek-owned Attica Enterpises, has acquired as its Scottish terminal a roll on/roll off berth at the former Royal Naval Dockyard, which the enterprising Forth Ports plc is also developing successfully as a port of call for many famous luxury ocean liners.

This book spotlights the ports on the Forth from Anstruther at its mouth to old Stirling on its upper reaches and tells of many of the ships and sailors who down through the centuries to the present day have helped contribute to their success and prosperity.

One

The Upper Forth

From Stirling to Bo'ness

The availability of sea transport provided by the River Forth was one of the main reasons that in 1759 a spot on the shores of its tributary, the Carron, was chosen as the site for Scotland's first large scale iron works. Carron became one of the world's first internationally recognised firms and to supply it with raw materials and to carry its products from canons to kitchen ranges to markets world wide it soon acquired its own shipping line. This boldly printed postcard advertised Carron Line's regular weekly overnight sailings from both Grangemouth and Bo'ness to London.

The 263 ton SS *Grange* was one of Carron Shipping Line's passenger vessels which provided a regular timetabled service between Grangemouth and London. This view shows her, with her single tall funnel and white railed promenade deck, setting sail from her home port. The *Grange* offered the choice of cabin class or steerage, the latter so called because its cheaper, more crowded accommodation was situated in the stern above the ship's propellers and rudder. Carron Line named many of its ships after rivers and other vessels in its fleet included the 554 ton *Avon*, the 389 ton *Derwent*, the 498 ton *Forth* and the 454 ton *Thames*. One Carron Line ship which broke with this tradition was the 255 ton *Margaret*. All of these vessels were registered at Grangemouth.

Other local passenger services plied daily the length of the Forth from Anstruther at the mouth of the Firth up as far as the tortuous, narrow, shallow windings of the river at Stirling as this view showing the paddle steamer, *Edinburgh Castle*, sailing through the Windings of the Forth depicts. The *Edinburgh Castle* was built for the Loch Goil & Loch Long Steamboat Co. on the upper Clyde by R. Duncan & Co. of Port Glasgow and launched in 1879. She was later purchased by Galloway Steam Packet Co. of Leith and transferred to the Forth where she entered service in 1886. At the beginning of the First World War, *Edinburgh Castle* was requisitioned by the Admiralty and was later converted into a hospital ship tender. She never returned to civilian use on the river.

(a different ship)

f e s

THE HARBOUR
STIRLING

As depicted in this rare postcard view of the port of Stirling, as well as small cargo sailing ships, it could adequately accommodate a vessel as large as one of Galloway Steam Ship Co.'s stylish paddle steamers. This is believed to be the same paddle steamer as seen in the previous photograph, the ~~Clyde-built~~ PS *Edinburgh Castle*. Passenger steam ship sailings on the Forth had begun as early as 1813 when steam pioneer Henry Bell brought his famous *Comet*, the world's first practical sea going vessel, through the Forth & Clyde Canal so that she could undergo her first annual overhaul at the shipbuilding yard of Shaw & Hart at Bo'ness, where he had himself served his apprenticeship. Upon its completion several local gentlemen paid the handsome sum of 7s 6d (37 1/2 pence) each for the privilege of sailing on her down river to Leith. The appearance of the *Comet*, with her tall black smoke stack and her paddle wheels set amidships created so much interest that by the following summer a group of local businessmen backed another Mr Bell, who was no relation of the inventor, to purchase another of the new-fangled steamers which had just been built and launched at Greenock to start a regular service on the Forth. Appropriately they named her the *Stirling* as she sailed daily between that inland port and Granton. She proved so successful that Mr Bell placed an order for the first two steamers to be built on the Forth. Constructed at Kincardine, or New Pans as it was formerly known because of its salt industry, the *Lady of the Lake* and *Morning Star* were launched on the same day. There were however not enough passengers for all three of his steamers and so Mr Bell had to sell his new *Morning Star* to German owners. Three years later however, trade had increased sufficiently for him to re-purchase the *Star* and she sailed all the way back from Hamburg down the Elbe and across the North Sea to the Forth. From 1818 until 1826 Mr Bell enjoyed a monopoly on the Forth, but that year he learned that several rival Stirling businessmen were proposing to put up the sum of £4,500 to found the rival Stirling, Alloa & Kincardine Steamboat Co. As a shrewd businessman Mr Bell offered to save them the trouble of building their own fleet by selling them his three vessels for exactly that amount. His offer was accepted and the new owners continued the monopoly of steamer traffic for almost ten years until it was challenged by a Mr Barclay, a Glasgow shipowner. He brought his ~~Benalmond~~ to the Forth and the result was a series of river boat battles which would not have disgraced the Mississippi. *Benlomond*

11

From the top of the Wallace Monument the famous Windings of the Forth, the torturous, twisting, turning narrows where rival paddle steamers used to vie are clearly visible. One such paddle steamer battle was immortalised by American travel writer, N.P.Willis, who wrote, 'The *Benalmond* and the *Victoria* on the latter of which I was a passenger got under way together from the quay at Stirling. The river was narrow and the tide down and the *Benalmond*, which seemed the better boat, was a little ahead as we approached a sharp bend in the course of the stream. *Victoria* however had the advantage of the inside of the course and very soon with the commencement of the curve we gained sensibly on the enemy. The narrowness of the river meant our paddle boxes almost touched as we swept past at a good twelve knots. To our utter amazement our pilot jammed down the tiller and rammed *Victoria*'s battered bow into the *Benalmond*'s forward quarter. Next moment we were going like mad down the middle of the river and far astern *Benalmond* was stuck in the mud, her paddles driving her deeper at every stroke.'

Stirling nowadays never sees vessels as large as the Victorian paddle steamers which, until the coming of the railways, provided its townsfolk with their fastest way of travelling to Edinburgh. It does however still have an enthusiastic boating club, whose headquarters is pictured in this postcard view taken during the 1910s.

The tiny harbour at Dunmore on the south shore of the Forth midway between Stirling and Kincardine, although much silted with mud, is still the base for small wooden-hulled, black painted vessels called cobbles from which salmon are caught using the hauf method of fishing in which a net is strung between the stern of the boat and the shore. Dunmore was built in Victorian times as a model village by Catharine, Countess of Dundonald, to house her estate workers. The stone built building beyond the pier was the village smiddy, or blacksmith's forge, where the farrier shod the horses; the work is still recalled by the unusual horse shoe-shaped entrance.(John Doherty)

1049. Alloa from the South

The former port of Alloa is seen from the south side of the Forth in this early picture postcard photograph. In the days in the 1700s when Scotland's roads were still in very poor condition, mere muddy quagmires in winter and rutted dust bowls during the summer months, Alloa's position so far up river gave it a great advantage as this allowed sea transport to deliver cargoes so far inland. The English author of *Robinson Crusoe*, Daniel Defoe, when he toured Scotland in the years prior to the Union of the Parliaments in 1707, was so impressed with the port that he wrote in the journal of his travels that, 'A merchant of Alloa may trade to all parts of the world.'

13

This postcard view shows the dock gates and the entrance to the port of Alloa. Thanks to the beer produced by its breweries and the bottles for it manufacured by its glass works, Alloa continued to prosper throughout the 1800s. In 1861 it was decided to transform the harbour by building a large new dock, 450ft long and 137ft broad with a depth of 24ft and a 50ft wide dock gate. The new dock also catered for the export of coal from the local collieries and the import of pit prop. Alloa closed as a port in the 1960s.

The import of pit props was the main trade at South Alloa, as seen in this late Victorian view. The pit prop trade was invented by George Stewart who, as a young clerk in the office of the Grange Colliery, Bo'ness, realised the need for underground supports following the abandonment of the old stack and room method of mining in favour of the more efficient Shropshire method (or longwall system). This meant that instead of leaving pillars of coal to support the workings all of the coal was mined, thus creating the need for pit props, as they became known. George Stewart's career and the shipping line he founded are described later. South Alloa continued for longer as a port than Alloa and small tankers continued to discharge at its oil terminal until the mid-1980s, their calls at it resulting in the last openings of the Kincardine Bridge.

Kincardine, on the Fife shore, was formerly known as New Pans because of its salt making industry. The evaporation of salt water from the Forth to produce salt could only take place where there was a ready source of coal and the pans at Kincardine were the furthest inland. As at Alloa, there was also a small shipbuilding yard. The pier is still used by a number of fishing boats and there is also a second pier a short distance farther down river at Longannet Power Station.

When opened in 1936 Kincardine on Forth Road Bridge was the furthest point down river where it was possible to cross the Forth by road. Nicknamed 'The Silver Link', it replaced the ferry from Higgensneuk on the Stirlingshire shore to Kincardine. Coats of arms above the portcullis gates on either side of the swing span depict the crests of Stirlingshire and Clackmannanshire as Kincardine was at that time in the latter. The bridge had its own fire-fighting unit and there was a lifeboat on the engine room level closest to the river surface. With its 364ft long central swing span it is still the world's longest swing bridge, although decline in river traffic means that it has not been opened for over a decade and is no longer manned twenty-four hours a day. The bridge functioned faultlessly for over fifty years, a fine tribute to its designer J. Guthrie Brown, C.B.E. of Sir Alexander Gibb & Co., and also to the Bridge Masters and ten man crews responsible for its operation. Each opening was co-ordinated from a bridge like that on a liner, situated above the road deck. First openings in 1936 took thirty minutes but through practice this time was cut to eleven minutes. Once in motion the bridge was carried through its swing by its own momentum so it was economical to operate, originally costing only 6d (2½p) in electricity each opening. To ensure equal wear and tear on both ends of the swing span it was turned through half a revolution every Sunday morning at 6 a.m., which was the quietest time for road traffic. The bridge is so congested that a second bridge is to be built 200 metres up river and when completed one way traffic will operate.

Longannet with its record breaking tall chimney, which is in fact four smoke stacks wrapped in one and is the largest of its type in Europe, is seen on the Fife shore in this aeriel view of Grangemouth Docks on the opposite shore of the river. On the left of the photograph the mud silted River Carron is seen flowing into the Forth with the Grange Burn, from which the town took its name flowing into the river on the opposite side of the modern dock entrance lock. In the fore ground is the oil tank farm of the giant Grangemouth petro-chemical complex. The complex is the largest payer of local council tax in the country and the oil refinery belonging to British Petroleum is the only one in Scotland. Crude oil is pumped directly to it through a pipe line from the North Sea, which comes ashore three miles further down river at Kinneil Bay.

This second aeriel view of Grangemouth Docks was taken from the opposite direction looking from the north over the whole of the port. The first dock entrance directly from the Forth can be seen in the centre foreground with the new larger entrance lock on the left. Forming the boundaries of the port, the muddy courses of the Grange Burn on the left and the River Carron on the right snake inland through the New and Old Towns of Grangemouth respectively. The oil and liquid petroleum gas tanks of the Grangemouth refinery can be clearly seen with the tanks of the Common User Jetty clustered between the dock basin and the east bank of the River Carron in the centre of the picture. The distance from the dock gates to the centre of Grangemouth is over two and a half miles.

The original entrance to the port of Grangemouth was from the River Carron, where this squat white-washed lighthouse guided vessels to the dock gates. The vessel in the picture is the SS *Orient*.

Grangemouth was originally known as Sealock as it first came into existence when it was chosen to be the eastern terminal of the Forth & Clyde Canal on which work began in July 1768. The canal, whose entrance lock is seen in this early postcard photograph, runs from Grangemouth to Bowling on the Clyde but was originally to have entered the Forth five miles further down river at the exisitng port of Bo'ness from where work commenced with a section dug to the west. Stirlingshire estate owner Laurence Dundas, however, foresaw the trade which this trans-Scotland waterway would undoubtably bring and used all of his business finesse and influence to persuade the canal company to resite the eastern sea lock on his land, thus giving birth to the port which is now the second most important in Scotland.

1768 ? — 1790 ?

alan meep 2/

Grangemouth was originally a tidal harbour and vessels using it were left high and dry at low tide as seen in this picture of early sailing and steam vessels. The ship in the foreground, like many which docked at Grangemouth, came from the Netherlands and the presence of the crews of these vessels together with flatness of the reclaimed land upon which the town was built and its canal all helped earn it the nickname of Little Holland.

This early postcard view shows Junction Dock and the first lock of the Forth & Clyde Canal. The thirty-five-mile-long canal, whose re-opening is Scotland's largest Millennium Lottery funded project, was designed by John Smeaton. Begun in 1790 it took teams of labourers, many of them from Ireland and others from the north of Scotand seeking work after the Highland clearances, twenty-two years to complete, including the Monkland Canal which linked it to the Glasgow hinterland and the Lanarkshire coal fields and thus added greatly to its commercial success. The labourers were known as 'navvies' as they were said to navigate the channel as they dug it right across the narrow waist of central Scotland to Bowling on the Clyde.

From the Junction Lock the Forth & Clyde Canal stretched west and here the first quarter mile of the waterway is seen running through the heart of what became known as Grangemouth Old Town, above whose dockers' homes can be seen the cranes of the Grangemouth Dockyard Co. The layout of the Old Town was meticulously planned by Sir Laurence Dundas as a model town. In his original layout the roads (including Canal Street seen in this photograph) were intended to form the shape of a sailing ship. He died before his idea was achieved, but his son carried through most of his other ideas regarding the width and straightness of the streets and the quality of the working class homes which lined them. Grangemouth prosperd to such an extent that in 1861 the Dundas family decided to start what became known as the New Town stretching from the canal east to the Grange Burn.

A 'puffer' steams along the Forth & Clyde Canal at Grangemouth after discharging its cargo at the port. 'Puffers' similar to this one were built on the canal at Kirkintilloch. The canal was also the first place in Britain where a steel-hulled vessel operated. She was appropriately named the *Vulcan*. In this picture the canal bridge has been opened to allow the 'puffer' to sail through and, to the right, the round toll house where vehicles using the bridge had to pay dues can also be seen.

The Forth & Clyde Canal, seen pictured in this view with North Basin Street in the background, was completed in 1790 and Grangemouth's harbour became so popular with ships able to unload their cargoes straight into canal barges ready for onward transportation across Central Scotland that it was soon successful in its application for its own Custom House. This was a significant development as it made the new port entirely independent of neighbouring Bo'ness. Grangemouth's trading dominance continued in the 1840s and 1850s when the coming of the railway superseded the canal as the preferred means of inland transport because, with the flatness of the new port, much of whose land was reclaimed from the waters of the River Forth, it was much easier to build the new tracks than at Bo'ness which was tightly hemmed in by the old steep raised beaches of the Forth. The new, undeveloped, spacious, flat site which Grangemouth occupied was also far more appealing than the already crowded coastal strip at Bo'ness to the the new industries which were established along the shores of the Forth in Victorian times and the early decades of the last century. In the end in 1959 the British Transport Commission closed the docks at Bo'ness, leaving Grangemouth to prosper as Scotland's second most important seaport.

By Victorian times Grangemouth was a bustling port. On the left the scene is dominated by the clock tower of the first town hall, which still stands along with the now derelict Queens Hotel, which in its hey day was the poshest of Grangemouth's many taverns where captains of ships in the docks often arranged to meet their shore agents, both to discuss business and to enjoy a drink. Opposite the porticoed facade of the Queens can be seen a large tall stack of Baltic timber which was one of Grangemouth's most important imports. The shops in the Old Town included several drapers selling uniforms and ships chandlery including that of the author's grandfather, local councillor and magistrate Baillie William Fyfe Hendrie, after whom he is named.

Portonians, as the people of Grangemouth are known, made full use of the facilities which the canal and the town's four rivers offered by using them for sport and relaxation. Here large crowds of enthusiastic townsfolk are seen gathered to cheer on the competitors in a local summer regatta.

Regattas on the Forth & Clyde Canal at Grangemouth also used frequently to feature very popular novelty events including walking the greasy pole in which nautical skills were no doubt put to good use as seen in this photograph.

As Scotland's second most important seaport the history of Grangemouth Docks dates back to 1843 when the Forth & Clyde Canal Co. decided that it was no longer acceptable to have vessels left high and dry at low tide. As a result the first proper dock was built. The first ship to sail through the lock gates was the SS *Hampton*. The steamer had had to lie off in the river since her arrival on the previous Friday because of problems with the new dock gates but six days later her entry into the dock went without a hitch. As she berthed with the help of the steam paddle tug, *Harmony*, she was greeted by the firing of several small cannon and the enthusiastic cheers of a 5,000 strong crowd. By 1855 it was decided that a second dock was required. Named the Junction Dock, it was opened in October 1859. For several years the Caledonian Railway had been eager to acquire a port on the east coast but it took until 1877 to complete a deal with the canal company. The outcome was the excavation of the Carron Dock which covered an area of 19½ acres. The entrance lock was 350ft long with a depth of 26ft of water and the dock opened on 3 June 1882. It had the most modern cranes and hydraulic coal hoists. Coal was Grangemouth's largest export and each hoist could cope with eighty-five railway wagon loads each day. In October 1898 work began on the very large Carron Dock. The most modern dredgers from the Netherlands, known locally as 'Dutch Blowers', were used. Progress was slow and the opening was delayed until October 1906. Salvesen Line's RMS *Norway* was the first vessel to enter the dock, her bows breaking a blue ribbon as they passed through the gates. In 1914 the port was requisitioned by the Admiralty and named HMS *Rameses* under the command of Admiral L. Clinton Baker. Among the naval vessels based in the docks were the famous Q Ships under Commander Campbell. These were camouflaged merchant ships carrying concealed guns and they acted as decoys to try to lure enemy U-boats into attacking them.

The port re-opened to commercial shipping in December 1918 and during the 1920s-1930s trade continued to expand until the outbreak of war in 1939 caused a set back. After peace returned the election of a Labour government resulted in the port being nationalised under the control of the British Transport Commission. During this period oil replaced timber as the main import. Another major change occurred in May 1966 when Grangemouth became the first port in Britain to be able to handle containers with the erection of two huge twenty-five ton hoists later replaced by more powerful ones capable of lifting forty tons Around this time it was also provided with a ro-ro berth which enabled tractors produced at the British Leyland plant at Blackburn near Bathgate to roll onto ferries for export while similar vessels brought imports of foreign cars.

Now owned by Forth Ports plc, Grangemouth continues to be known as one of the country's most efficient ports with a dedicated work force capable of producing the fastest possible turn rounds for all types of vessels from oil tankers to liquid petroleum gas tankers and from box ships to bulk carriers. (Arthur Down)

A shipping company with close links with Grangemouth was the Gibson Rankine Line, whose well-known skipper Captain Mercer Scobbie is pictured here. When he was not at sea, Captain Scobie lived with his wife Nancy at home in Grangemouth where they resided for many years at Garfield House, which still stands in Abbotsgrange Road. The Gibson Line was founded in 1820 by George Gibson who had previously been the manager of the Leith, Hamburg & Rotterdam Shipping Co. Until 1850 Gibson Line operated sailing vessels but in that year ordered its first steamship. She was named *Balmoral*. In 1870 the launch of the *Abbotsford*, named after Sir Walter Scott's Borders home near Melrose, began a tradition of naming the company's vessels after the author's books and places connected with him. The company was taken over in 1972 by the famous Anchor Line, but the name George Gibson & Co. was retained to manager a fleet of small gas tankers which still bore names such as *Quentin*, *Teviot* and *Traquair*.

Amongst the vessels of the Gibson Rankine Line of which Captain Scobbie was skipper was the SS *Grangemouth*, which is seen here with her tall black funnel. the merger of Gibson Line and Rankine Line took place in 1920 following the death of the last member of the Gibson family who was killed in action during the First World War. The Rankine Line had been founded by Glasgow merchant James Rankine and, as well as existing routes in European waters, the merged company expanded to serve the Far East.

This early photograph shows the port of Grangemouth as it looked shortly after the completion of the Carron Dock in 1882. The dock was named after the River Carron, up which vessels had to sail to enter it through an entrance lock. Although not used for a century the lock survives and is still used as one of the port's dry docks. The Carron Dock, which occupies a twenty-acre site, can accommodate vessels with a draught up to 25ft.

The largest of Grangemouth's docks, the thirty-acre Grange Dock is pictured here shortly before its completion in 1906. On the left is the swing bridge constructed to span the channel dug to connect it with the older Carron Dock, seen in the previous photograph.

A steamer discharges cargo in the Grange Dock shortly after its completion in 1906. Notice the large coal hoists on the quayside on the left. During the early years of the twentieth century Grangemouth was a popular bunkering port for steamers as they knew that they could always rely on plentiful supplies of good coal which came mainly from the Lanarkshire coalfield. It was brought by rail to Grangemouth which was equipped with the very latest thirty-six ton coal hoists.

During fueling operations each ship was served by two of these powerful hoists which, as this photograph shows, were capable of emptying the entire contents of a coal wagon in one speedy operation.

loading for export - bunkers had small openings

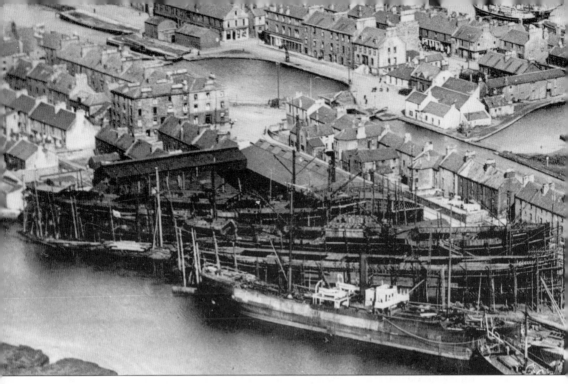

One of Grangemouth's industries was shipbuilding and the Grangemouth Dockyard Co. became one of the best known yards on the Forth or, to be strictly accurate, the Carron because it was into this narrow muddy tributary that it had the difficult task of launching the vessels which it built. Viewed from the south west across the Carron several vessels are seen under construction.

Grangemouth was involved in the whale oil industry between the years 1850 and 1870, but this was not one of the whales caught during a voyage to the Arctic. It was in fact landed on the quayside during the 1920s after it swam up the Forth and became trapped in the docks. Despite efforts to save it, the whale died and its disposal posed a considerable problem for the local authorities. Another whale swam through the entrance lock and entered the docks during the 1950s. It became trapped and died in the entrance to the canal. A century earlier the blubber of the whales caught by the Grangemouth Arctic fishers was boiled for oil at a small refinery near Nelson Street. During the 1960s Grangemouth enjoyed its fastest decade of growth as it became an oil boom town with the enormous growth of its BP Oil Refinery and associated industries. The town's connection with oil came in the 1930s when Scottish Oils, which refined shale rock in West and Mid Lothian, decided to import crude oil from the Persian Gulf. Grangemouth was selected as the most convenient port to discharge the first cargoes of foreign oil on the basis that if the venture proved uneconomic the new refinery built there could easily revert to processing crude from the local shale industry. Today the raw material for the BP Refinery at Grangemouth comes once more from the North Sea, not in the form of blubber from whales, but as crude oil delivered by the pipe line which comes ashore at Kinneil Bay.

near Peterhead

The most famous vessel constructed at Grangemouth was also one of the earliest, the pioneering *Charlotte Dundas*, which was the world's first practical steamship. Launched in 1801, eleven years before the Clyde-built *Comet*, she was designed by Dumfriesshire inventor William Symington. He enjoyed the patronage of Lord Dundas of Kerse who persuaded him that his innovative vessel should be constructed at Grangemouth so that her trials could take place on the canal. The *Charlotte Dundas* was 56ft long with a beam of 18ft and drew 8ft. She cost £7,000 to construct and equip with a steam engine with a cylinder of 22in diameter. The piston drove a stern wheel. During experimental voyages which took place throughout 1802 and 1803 the *Charlotte Dundas* proved powerful enough to tow two fully laden 70 ton barges, the *Active* and the *Euphemia*. The canal authorities became concerned that the wash from the steamer's stern paddle wheel was damaging the banks and ordered a halt to the trials. The *Charlotte Dundas* was laid up at Bainsford and never sailed again. She is still remembered in Grangemouth through her inclusion as a proud symbol on the town's coat of arms.

The familiar profile of the distinctive offices of the Grangemouth Dockyard Co. seen here reflected in the still waters of the Forth & Clyde Canal, long before it was filled in to make way for a road. In this picture the dockyard was at its busy height with the crane towering over the bows of a large cargo vessel taking shape on the stocks. Once completed, the Grangemouth yard launched its vessels into the River Carron. The narrowness of the Carron added to the trickiness of this operation as ships had to be launched sideways into the water.

The dockyard was decked with flags to mark the occasion of the launch of the cargo ship SS *Gannet*, which had just been completed on the stocks and was about to be launched. Of particular interest is the large banner in the foreground which, as well as the Union flag and the Lion Rampant, displays the yard's name and the symbols for Grangemouth including the antlered deer and the *Charlotte Dundas*, whose construction was the yard's first claim to fame.

The cargo ship *Palomares* is seen nearing completion on the stocks at the Grangemouth Dockyard Co. The Grangemouth yard built many cargo vessels for foreign owners including several in Malta, Portugal and Iceland.

Riveters, platers and other workers at the Grangemouth Dockyard Co. all wearing their flat bunnets waited patiently at the end of their shift on Friday afternoons to receive their weeks wages in cash. Money for the wage packets was collected by the office staff each Friday morning and paid out later in the day through the windows of the company's offices in Canal Street, different trades being paid at different windows.

Carron Dry Dock was created out of the original entrance from the River Carron.

Left: Ship repairs also kept the Grangemouth yard steadily occupied. In this Edwardian photograph the foreign sailing vessel *Ida IV*, registered in Groningen in the Netherlands, is seen in the yard's dry dock. The recession in the British shipbuilding industry in the 1960s and 1970s brought to an end shipbuilding in Grangemouth as it did to every shipbuilding yard on the Scottish east coast, but ship repairing still takes place at Grangemouth.

Below: The largest steel sheet ever exported from Grangemouth is seen being raised by crane from the quayside during the 1930s as some of the port's dockers looked on. Manufactured at Colville's steel works at Motherwell, it was transported by rail to Grangemouth where it was handled by local stevedoring firm, David Trail & Sons, who were in competition with Palmers & Simpson and Sharp. According to the statistics painted onto the steel this huge sheet weighed 15 tons, measured a massive 47ft 8in by over 13ft 7in and was over a foot thick. (Isabel McNab)

Described as a rotor ship, the *Buckau* attracted the attention of the photographer as this was her first call at Grangemouth. Rotor was an early word denoting that the vessel was turbine-powered.

Another unusual visitor to Grangemouth was this lifeboat which sailed through the Forth & Clyde Canal. Although such an important seaport Grangemouth has never possessed its own lifeboat, the nearest being the inshore vessel fifteen miles down river at the Hawes Pier, Queensferry.

During the years following the Second World War railway wagons were slowly replaced by road transport as shown in this busy dock scene. (Forth Ports plc)

This Hapag-Lloyd Line ship was one of the first to bring containers to Grangemouth, but there is also still much general cargo on the quayside waiting to be loaded. (Forth Ports plc)

Seen here sailing through the new entrance lock to the port the *Doulos* was an unusual visitor to Grangemouth during the 1980s. This former passenger ship was one of two vessels specially converted by an evangelical Christian organisation into a floating Bible bookshop. Her smaller sister ship the *Logos* also visited the port. During their stays in Grangemouth docks they were open to the public to raise funds both through the sale of books and from the proceeds of guided tours to provide money for their more usual visits to underdeveloped countries in Africa, South America and the West Indies.

Two decades earlier, another passenger liner that docked at Grangemouth on several occasions was the British India Line schoolship, *Dunera*, which on each occasion embarked over 1000 Scottish pupils for educational cruises to Norway and the Baltic countries. The 12,620 ton *Dunera*, which was built in 1937 as a troopship, paid her final call at Grangemouth in July 1967 shortly before she was withdrawn from service in October of that year to be replaced by SS *Uganda* which went on to gain fame as a hsopital ship during the Falklands War. (Forth Ports plc)

In the previous photograph tugs are seen guiding the *Doulos* through the entrance lock. The *Dundas* and the *Forth*, the 187 ton tug boats which serve the port of Grangemouth were owned originally by the Forth Towing Co. Now under Dutch ownership they are seen here in the new livery of the Muller Co., but still happily have been allowed to retain their local names. (Arthur Down)

A small box ship approaches the container berth which with its forty ton hoists was the first to offer such facilities in Scotland. Vessels like the one pictured here provide a regular service to Rotterdam where the containers are transferred to larger box ships for delivery across the Atlantic to the USA and worldwide. (Arthur Down)

R. M. S. Scotland, Dock Gates, Grangemouth.

Dressed over all the Royal Mail Steamer *Scotland* sails out of the port of Grangemouth at the start of one of her voyages across the North Sea to Norway. The trim little *Norway* with her graceful almost yacht-like lines was one of the fleet of vessels belonging to the famous Salvesen Line. Owned by a Norwegian family, Salvesens is usually more associated with Leith, but the company's earliest connections with Scotland were in fact through the port of Grangemouth when the young Christian Salvesen came to work there during the 1840s. In 1853 he moved to Leith and became a British citizen in 1859. At its height Salvesens had one of the largest fleets registered in Scotland with over thirty vessels and expanded its operations still further when, at the start of the twentieth century, using converted steam trawlers it sent a whaling expedition to Antarctica where it established a base which it called Leith Harbour in the icy wastes of South Georgia. At the start of the First World War Salvesen was the first Leith owner to loose a ship when its *Giltra* was sunk in the North Sea by a German U-boat, but only after the captain and crew had been allowed to take to the lifeboats. Until this time Salvesen's colours were red, white and black but this was now deemed too similar to those of the enemy and so the funnels of its vessels were repainted red, white and blue (a distinctive colour scheme which combined Norway's national colours and those of Great Britain and which in the interwar years became familiar world wide). During the Second World War, Salvesen again suffered losses, including their oil tanker *Salvestra*. Originally designed to carry whale oil from the Antarctic, early in 1940 she was diverted to the USA to load a vitally needed cargo of petrol. Fully laden she survived the Atlantic crossing, but on 27 July was destroyed in an explosion within sight of her home port of Leith when she struck a German mine 2.8 miles off the island of Inch Keith. The 500ft long vessel, which had a beam of 62ft, sank within minutes and fuel from her tanks was washed up on beaches on both shores of the Firth, but her loss was censored and not made public.

This is all that remains of the port of Culross *Blair pier* on the Fife shore, which in the Middle Ages was one of the most prosperous in Scotland. The merchants of Culross exported heavy cargoes of coal and salt mainly to the Netherlands and instructed the skippers of their vessels to use the profits (or 'light money' as they described it) to purchase imports of spices such as pepper and nutmeg and silks and other rich clothes brought home by the Dutch East India Co. These high value luxury goods could be easily stored in the wooden kist in the captain's cabin. Rather than leave the holds empty or return with unprofitable ballast, they were routinely filled with red pantiles (whose colourful hue still adds a distinctive touch to houses in Culross and all along the shores of the Forth) as well as blue and white Delft tiles. Iron was also imported at a time when Scotland produced only very small quantities of its own and this was used by the Hammermen of Culross, the local blacksmiths, who were so skilled at the production of baking girdles that they were granted a monopoly for their manufacture by King James VI. The Hammerman, whose symbol still appears on the town's coat of arms, guarded this privilege very jealously and reported the smiths in neighbouring Low Valleyfield when they dared to breach it. (Arthur Down)

James VI came to the Royal and Ancient Burgh, on his only return visit to Scotland after becoming James I of England in 1603. This royal visit took place in 1617 and during it James inspected the Moat Pit which the town's largest local landowner and industrialist George Bruce had constructed in the middle of Culross Bay so that cargoes of coal could be brought up its shaft and emptied straight into the holds of waiting small sailing vessels which exported it to continental markets. Pictured here is Bruce's home where the king stayed during his visit. Bruce was later knighted and proudly added the letter S for Sir to the G and the B which were carefully carved on the dormers of the windows in the newer part of his home. (Arthur Down)

This turreted town house with its white harled walls was the home of another Culross merchant and the tiny attic window to which he climbed to see if he could catch an early glimpse of one of his vessels returning from a successful foreign voyage can be seen below the red pantiled roof. Now known as the Study, because it later became home to the learned Bishop Leighton, it is now the home of the National Trust of Scotland's representative in the town, where the Trust has helped to preserve most of the buildings under its very successful Little Houses Scheme since they became its first acquisitions upon its foundation in 1932. (Arthur Down)

The National Trust for Scotland's headquarters in Culross is the burgh's former Town House, which overlooks the Sandgate where goods landed at the harbour opposite used to be weighed. The site of the weighing scales can still be seen in front of the unusual double stairs which led to the council chambers. The building with its distinctive curved Dutch belfry was also used as the town's court where rowdy, drunk or disorderly sailors were usually sentenced to be flogged with the leather last by the public executioner at the market cross. The executioner was also responsible for public hangings and the even more horrific burnings at the stake. This latter fate was usually reserved for the local witches who, when imprisoned before their trials, were always held in the attic cells whose tiny windows can be seen above the entrance, rather than in the basement prison in case it allowed them to communicate with their master, the Devil. (Arthur Down)

What happened to Charlestown, Bruce Haven

Directly opposite Culross on the south shore of the Forth lies Bo'ness, whose name is a shortened version of Borrowstounness, meaning the Burgh Town on the Ness or nose of land jutting out into the river. Until well into Victorian times, Bo'ness was a tidal port, with the ships which used it left high and dry on the mud in the harbour at low tide. The boom in coal exports in the middle of the nineteenth century and the establishment of the town as the headquarters of the pit prop importing business meant that much better facilities were required. With the support of the North British Railway, whose line had reached Bo'ness in 1851, the Town Commissioners, who were the early forerunners of the Town Council, therefore began the excavation of a wet dock. This considerable construction was finally completed in 1881 and massive wooden dock gates ensured that there was always sufficient water in the new dock to keep vessels safely afloat. At the highest spring tides, the depth of water at the dock entrance was 24ft. The new dock covered an area of $7\frac{1}{2}$ acres and offered a total of 2,400 yards of quay space. It was equipped with the latest hydraulic cranes and specially designed coal hoists. These latter were used both for the export of coal and for bunkering, that is the fueling of steamships. When the coal hoists rumbled on right through the night, the townsfolk knew that Bo'ness was prospering. The coal business became so brisk that Bo'ness became the second most important coaling port in Scotland. At the same time that the docks opened, the original harbour was also greatly improved by the extension of the East and West Piers, which each stretched 566ft out into the River Forth. Twice weekly the steamships of the famous Carron Co. provided a passenger service to London and the vessels of Stewart & Love & Co. and Denholm Ltd. had Bo'ness as their home port of registration.

Tall-masted sailing ships crowded the quays of the newly opened Bo'ness dock in the 1880s. There was a narrow walkway from one side of the docks to the other across the top of the massive wooden dock gates, which ensured that there was always a constant level of water for ships in the port. The dock gates had to be regularly maintained and the appearance of the diver in his massive, heavily weighted suit always brought crowds of onlookers to watch him at work. The huge iron capstan on the far quay was used to help pull ships into the dock. Goods landed from the vessels were stored in the warehouse, which can be seen behind the ships' rigging.

The dock warehouse can be seen more clearly in this elegant view of the docks taken about ten years later in the 1890s, when sail was gradually giving way to steam. The two be-hatted gentlemen standing on the quay wall appear to have been on an official inspection, accompanied by one of the local police constables wearing his navy frock coat and tall helmet. The buoy in the centre of the dock was used to moor ships awaiting a berth when all the quays were occupied. One of the port's coal hoists can be seen, behind the tall funnel of the steamer at the right hand berth.

Flat-capped local youths stared out across the harbour at the three tall masts of this very large sailing ship, whose bulk hid all but the slate roof of the Bo'ness Custom House. The deck of the sailing ship was crowded with people as if she was acting as a grandstand for one of the regattas, which were a popular feature of the Bo'ness summer scene. Alongside the sailing ship lay one of the new-fangled paddle steamers. In the background can be seen some of the houses on the braes behind the town including the fine Victorian villas built by the town's shipowners and merchants including the Denholms, Harrowers and Stewarts, which now form a protected conservation area. During both world wars Bo'ness dock was requisitioned by the Admiralty and on both occasions after peace was declared, trade was slow to recover. After the Second World War, competition from the better facilities available a short distance up river at Grangemouth, combined with the always present problem of silting caused by the notorious Forth mud, and the increased cost of dredging, finally led to the official closure by its owners, the British Transport Commission, in 1959.

The harbour's position in Bo'ness can be seen clearly in this earlier photograph of the town taken before the extension of the East and West Piers in 1881. The railway station opened in 1851 can be seen in the middle of the picture. It appears much closer to the shore than the site is nowadays because land reclamation had not yet taken place. The railway track was extended from the station in Corbiehall to the dock when it was opened in 1881 and a Parliamentary Act ordered the North British Railway to pay £150 per annum compensation to the townsfolk for their loss of right of access to the foreshore.

Three of the steam paddle tugs belonging to Captain Wilson, which were based at Bo'ness, can be spotted in this 1890s view of the harbour, but sail still predominated amongst the cargo ships berthed alongside its crowded quays. The Old Town Hall Clock Tower, the steeple of Craigmailen Church immediately to its left and the warehouses in East Pier Street can all be identified in the background.

Three large cargo steamers with their tall smoke stacks crowd the south quay of Bo'ness dock in this 1930s view of the port.

This postcard picture entitled 'Leaving Bo'ness' is a reminder that to assist vessels sailing out off and docking the port had its own steam tug and its own pilot. The pilot at the time the new dock opened was the author's Great Grandfather, Captain Matthew McBain, who in 1890 had the honour to be the first to bring a steamer up river under the completed Forth Railway Bridge. Shortly afterwards his devotion to duty cost him his life. On a bitterly cold, windy, rain-lashed, winter night, despite being already soaked to the skin after bringing one ship into port, he insisted on going back out in his open pilot cutter to bring in a second vessel, so that she would not have to weather the storm lying off out in the roads. By the time he finished he had caught pneumonia, a fatal chest illness in those days. In addition to their own six small children he left the author's Great Grandmother alone to bring up the son of his best friend, who had drowned. Young Robert Miller was the only one of the seven children, to follow in the author's Great Grandfather's wake. He went to sea, gained his master's ticket and emigrated to Australia. There he founded Miller Line, which with its oil tankers and bulk coal carriers is now one of the country's largest shipping lines.

As well as the harbour at the dock, there was also a small harbour a short distance further down river at Bridgeness. It was here that the boats bringing eggs from the Orkney Islands usually berthed. A crane can be seen on the quayside at the harbour mouth. It was this little harbour, which was later taken over by the ship-breaking yard of P. & W. McLellan, where many fine ships were broken up. P. & W. McLellan also had a smaller yard further east at Carriden. Two other Bo'ness industries can be seen in this 1890s photo. The large work's chimney in the foreground was that of Thomson & Balfour's Victoria Sawmill, while the one from which the smoke puffs was that of the Grange Colliery. Coal wagons can be seen waiting to be loaded.

Bo'ness dockers posed on the railway track on the quayside for the cameraman in front of the funnel and lifeboat of one of the steamers that they were loading in this 1890s photograph. Notice how young the two boys were. Children were still allowed to leave school to go to work when they were only twelve years old. It is interesting to observe that even the little boy apprentice dockers, like their elders, wore flat caps. The foreman in charge, who is seated in the middle of the front row, can be picked out by his bowler hat and the crane-man is seated on the steps below the door and two windows of the cabin of his hoist.

Left: The pit prop trade was one of the most prosperous in Bo'ness. It was indeed the invention of George Stewart, a young clerk at the Grange Colliery who went onto to become the Provost of the town. While working over the ledgers in his office at the pithead, young Stewart became conscious that at the beginning of each shift the miners used up a lot of time selecting and trimming the timber supports which had become necessary to support the underground working since the abandonment of the old stack and room method and its replacement by the Shropshire or Longwall System. He therefore had the brainwave to start importing ready-cut pit props of the correct length from the abundant soft wood pine forests of the Scandinavian and Baltic countries. So successful did this business become that, in partnership with a Glasgow business man called Love, he founded his own shipping line whose most famous vessel was the *Lovart*, a neat combination of both of their names and Bo'ness went on to become the pit prop capital of the world, nicknamed Pitpropalis, or more simply Prop Town. Prop yards stretched forest-like along the shores of the River Forth from Kinneil in the west to Carriden in the east. From April when the thawing of the Baltic ice made it possible for the prop boats to bring fresh supplies from the Baltic countries and from as far away as Russia, it was said that it was possible to smell Bo'ness before you saw it because of the sweet perfume of the resin oozing from timber.

In contrast to the dockers in their workaday clothes on the previous page, this docker is dressed in his best Sunday suit for this very posed picture. Taken on a summer Sunday it appropriately also shows the town's original Free Kirk, now the Bo'ness United Social Club, and several of the substantial, stone-built houses can also be seen on the hillside above the then recently built St Andrew's Free Church on Grange Terrace. Behind the docker can be seen the tall chimneys and slate-roofed buildings of Ballantyne's Foundry at the foot of Links Brae. The foundry is still in production and, apart from moulded manhole covers, its very varied products include fireplace surrounds illustrated with scenes from the famous Elgin Marbles, for which it holds the sole rights, spiral wrought iron staircases and replica cannons, some of which grace the battlements of Edinburgh Castle. (Photo by kind permission of John Doherty)

Members of the United General Sea Box Society of Borrowstounness pose on the steps of Seamore. The house in Grange Terrace was later bought by John Cochrane, the bearded gentleman at the extreme left of the front row, who also later became president of the society for a period of twenty-seven years. He renamed his new home 'Rondebush', after the district of Capetown, South Africa, where he had enjoyed working as a young man, before returning to lead the family's prosperous engineering firm in Bo'ness. The Sea Box, which is the oldest institution of its kind in the world, is still in existence. It was founded over 360 years ago by the skippers of the Bo'ness sailing ships, who after each successful voyage, promised to put a proportion of their profits into a big, double-locked, wooden kist. This fund provided benefits for their seamen and their families in the form of a local welfare state, centuries before the national one was introduced in 1948. As well as helping local seafaring families with sickness benefits, pensions and even death grants to pay for their funerals, the Sea Box also on occasion helped foreign, distressed mariners ranging from those who had been shipwrecked to those who had been held captive and tortured by the pirates of the Barbary Coast. The fine model sailing ship still sails high in the air in the Sailors' Loft at Bo'ness Old Kirk and the bell seen in front of it can be found in Kinneil Museum, along with the wooden sea box from which this venerable society takes its proud title. The members of the Sea Box continue to meet several times a year and one of their recent presidents was Mr William Cochrane, the grandson of the president in the picture. The Sea Box is still an all-male institution and Mr Cochrane's son-in-law, Grant Cuthell, now carries the family's long connection with this historic body forward to the next generation. (Picture by permission of Mr William Cochrane)

Tidings Hill took its name from the fact that it was to this vantage point high above the harbour at Bo'ness that wives and girlfriends made their way to try to be the first to catch sight of the town's Arctic Whaling fleet returning at the end of its long season in October. The mansion house was built by the Denholm family of shipowners who were closely connected with the development of the port.

This tranquil evening picture looks out over the placid waters of the dock. When the last vessel sailed away in 1959 a contemporary report stated that the heart had been ripped out of Bo'ness. Many of the town's older inhabitants still bitterly regret the closure of the port and remember fondly that Daniel Defoe wrote that the sailors of Bo'ness were, 'the best seamen in the Firth and good pilots for the coast of Holland, the Baltic and the coast of Norway.'

P. & W. McLellan's Bridgeness Ship-breaking Yard was pictured in this aerial view of the east end of Bo'ness. Ship-breaking first became established at Bridgeness in 1898 when the yard was established by Mr A. Turnbull. Six years later in 1904 it became known as The Forth Shipbreaking Co. It was soon successful in bidding for the demolition of several P&O and Cunard passenger liners, one of the most famous of which was the former Atlantic Blue Riband holder, *Umbria*, which was purchased for £20,000. She sailed from Liverpool on her last voyage to the Forth on 10 May 1910 and on the following Monday afternoon a first attempt was made to beach her at the yard. Crowds lined the south shore of the Forth, where large white sheets were hung to mark the spot where she was to be grounded and there was great excitement as the tall, red-funnelled Cunarder sailed up river past Bo'ness before swinging round to commence her final dash at full speed for the shore. All seemed well and she seemed on target until only 200 yards from the shore she hit mud and came to an abrupt halt. There she remained stuck fast throughout the entire summer while work proceeded on lightening her by stripping out her internal fittings until, in September, a spring tide enabled the 519 feet long vessel to be maneuvered alongside the waiting cranes. The Bo'ness yard was taken over by P. & W. McLellan's. The largest liner broken up during their fifty-year ownership of the Bridgeness Yard and of a neighbouring one a short distance further down river at Carriden was the SS *Columbia*, the impressive 27,000 ton three stacker seen in this view looking out over the river. The *Columbia* had a draught of 35ft and a special channel had to be dredged to enable her to be beached at the yard. A contemporary account of her last voyage states, 'Thick black smoke belched from two of her three funnels, when after lying off shore for two weeks awaiting the highest available tide, she set out on her final suicidal course for the shore. With a Forth pilot on the bridge she sailed down river almost as far as Crombie Point on the Fife side, before he requested her master to turn her bows towards Bridgeness where a huge square of sail cloth hung high from the tallest crane indicated where she was to be brought to rest. Turning shorewards at the Dodds Buoy there was an anxious moment when she touched bottom on a bank of mud and listed suddenly to starboard, but struggled free and came on at full speed towards the yard. Half a mile from the shore she again grounded but with a sudden thrust of power her propellers forced her forward and she reached the shore only feet from the spot which the breakers had marked for her. As her boilers blew off steam, her siren gave one long mournful blast and the engine room signal on the bridge sounded finished with engines for the very last time.'

The Canadian Pacific emigrant ship *Metagama*, which carried thousands of Scots across the Atlantic to Canada, was another famous passenger ship which eventually ended her days at Bo'ness. She completed her final voyage to the Forth in 1935 and this photograph was taken immediately after she was beached at P. & W. McLellans Bridgeness Yard with steam still puffing out of her for'ard funnel. The grounding of a vessel of this size always caused a miniature tidal wave, which swept across the road outside the yard. The raised step at the gate into the garden of Floral Cottage, designed to protect it from flood water, is still a reminder of this. Like many families in Bo'ness, the Cuthells who owned Floral Cottage often attended the auction of the contents of vessels scrapped at the ship-breakers. At one sale they bid for and acquired a magnificent grand piano from the first class sitting room of one of the liners, which was subsequently played by their talented musician son Jimmy.

Two

The Lower Forth

Blackness to the Forth Bridge

The most famous passenger liner scrapped in the Forth was undoubtedly the impressive four-funnelled Cunarder, *Mauretania* pictured here steaming up the Firth on her final voyage to the breakers in 1935. Built by Swan Hunter & Wigham Richardson on the Tyne in 1907, the magnificent 31,938 ton 'Maurie', as she was known affectionately, had a service speed of 25 knots. Powered by steam turbines the 790ft long, quadruple screw vessel was capable of carrying over 2,300 passengers. In her day she held the Blue Riband trophy for the fastest crossing of the Atlantic for more years than any other ship and was only displaced from her role by the arrival on the route of Cunard's new Clyde-built *Queen Mary*.

Aquitania, *Berengaria* and *Mauretania* made up Cunard Line's big three and here the latter dwarfs the old steam tug waiting to escort her to her final berth in the breaker's yard at Roysth near Dunfermline in Fife on the north shore of the Forth. (Nelson Patrick Hendrie)

To reach her last berth alongside the breakers' cranes at Rosyth, the mighty *Mauretania* had to sail beneath the cantilever spans of the equally muckle Forth Bridge and her tall masts had to be trimmed to allow her to do so. (Nelson Patrick Hendrie)

Mauretania makes the final turn into the breaker's yard just after the Forth Rail Bridge and is soon to be reduced to scrap metal. Souvenirs were made of her decking and it was turned in to all sorts of trinkets including barrels, letter openers and bookmarks.

The second Cunard liner *Mauretania*, launched on the Mersey by the Birkenhead yard of Cammel Laird in July 1938 also ended her days at breakers in the Forth, this time at the famous yard of Ward of Inverkeithing. Often known as the *Queen Elizabeth*'s first cousin she was one of the first casualties in the Cunard fleet of the arrival of jet aircraft and was withdrawn from service in November 1965. Weighing 35,655 tons, 772ft long and, with a beam of 89ft and a draft of 30ft, she could carry 1,140 passengers – 470 in first class, 370 in cabin class and 300 in tourist. She was decorated throughout in a late Art Deco style similar to that aboard RMS *Queen Elizabeth*. *Mauretania* was photographed here alongside the jetty at Ward's in the shadow of the Forth Railway Bridge, shortly before the breakers' hammers began to take their toll of her proud hull and superstructure. Twin screwed and powered by steam turbines she had a service speed of 23 knots. (Dr Louis Rusack)

A postcard view of St Margaret's Hope and Rosyth before it was developed during the First World War as Scotland's only Royal Naval Dockyard.

opened 1905

As well as merchant ships, the breakers at Rosyth also demolished naval vessels. Here is HMS *Benbow* being cut up at Metal Industries on 17 March 1931.

During the First World War the 12th and 13th Submarine Squadrons were repositioned from Scapa Flow south to Rosyth. The Royal Navy's submarine division had been founded only sixteen years earlier in 1901 and these two squadrons were both equipped with its most modern vessels, K-class submarines such as K6, which is seen in the photograph. Built by Vickers of Barrow in Furness in 1916 and 1917 the K-class submarines were the largest underwater craft then afloat and were powered while on the surface by steam turbines, which meant that they required funnels, which had to be lowered and stowed before the submarine could submerge. Late in the afternoon of 31 January 1918 as dusk settled over the river, nine of these strange-looking submarines set to sea from Rosyth to accompany Admiral Beatty's fleet on exercise in the North Sea. In flotilla they sailed below the Forth Bridge and as darkness fell sailed on down the Firth. Off the May Island they encountered a group of mine sweepers which, unaware of the exercise, sailed straight across the path of the sea going fleet. Trying to take avoiding action in the pitch darkness K22 hit K14, slicing off her bows. The battle cruiser HMS *Invincible* then collided with the already damaged bow of K22. The radio silence which had been imposed during the exercise was then broken and all vessels were ordered to display their navigation lights, but no message was transmitted to warn the on-coming ships that several of the vessels in the van of the fleet had by then changed course and were in the midst of turning. As a result the cruiser, HMS *Fearless* hit K17. Her crew managed to escape before she sank, but much worse was to follow. Her sister vessels K3 and K4 both stopped and this resulted in the latter being hit by K6, which almost sliced her in half. Locked together, the two submarines began to sink quickly and it was only by going astern that K6 managed to avoid being drawn under as K4 rolled over and sank, drowning all members of her ship's company. More lives were lost as the following surface vessels ploughed into the sailors from the other damaged submarines who were struggling in the water and the final death toll reached 100. The wrecks of K4 and K17 have never been raised and still lie about 55 metres down on the sea bed off the May as a memorial to this disaster.

Following the Armistice in 1918 the battleships, cruisers and destroyers of the German fleet were ordered to proceed to the Firth of Forth to tender their surrender. Escorted by the Royal Navy's Fifth Battle Squadron they sailed up river and this picture postcard captured the moment when the cruiser *Konigsberg* anchored down river from Queensferry to enable the German delegate to meet with Admiral Beatty. Following the meeting it was announced that all of the German vessels would leave their overnight anchorage the following day at noon to sail north to Scapa Flow, where they would be impounded, but as explained in the next caption their captains had other ideas.

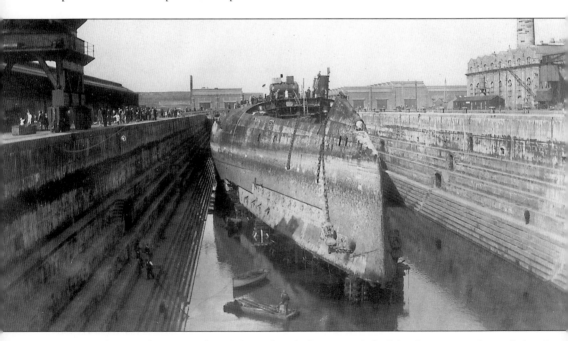

At Scapa Flow, on the secret orders of their admiral, the crews of all of the German vessels scuttled and sank their ships. During the 1920s and 1930s their wrecks were raised and towed south from Orkney to the Forth for scrapping. Often, as in this photograph, they were towed hull up, as this was the safest way for them to complete their final voyages, to the breakers at Rosyth.

Situated at the end of a long narrow peninsula of black basalt from which it derives its name, Blackness is often nicknamed Scotland's Ship Shape Castle. According to Historic Scotland its appearance as a thick stone-walled man o'war derived simply from the elongated shape of the site upon which it rises straight out of the waters of the Forth, but local tradition tells a more romantic tale. According to it Blackness was built by Archibald Douglas, the Lord High Admiral of the Scottish Fleet in the time of King James V, so that he could assure His Majesty that he was doing his duty aboard ship, without the risk of the violent seasickness from which he always suffered when he actually put to sea.

The ship-shape nature of Blackness Castle is seen to advantage in this picture taken from out in the river. All of the structures in the castle bear the names of parts of ships from the Stern Tower, where the governor had his spacious quarters, to the Main Mast Tower and the Fo'c'sle Tower, where prisoners were lodged in its damp dungeons.

Blackness was garrisoned until the 1920s and the recently fully restored pier was added in Victorian times when the castle became the army's principal ammunition store in Scotland. Landing ammunition direct from the sea at Blackness was considered much safer than transporting such dangerous loads overland in Scotland and the deck of the pier was made entirely of wood to lessen the risk of explosions which steel might have caused.

During Victorian times it was anticipated that Blackness would become a large holiday resort and this postcard view of boating in the village's east bay shows some of the potential it was felt to possess.

Tobacco featured amongst the exports from Blackness. As a result of the Navigation Acts which decreed that all exports from British colonies had to be carried in ships belonging to the colony of origin and be transported first to Britain, no matter where the eventual destination, tobacco from Virginia and other American sources was landed at Port Glasgow and then transported across Central Scotland to the nearest harbours on the east coast at Alloa, Bo'ness and Blackness from where it was re-exported to the Netherlands for cigar manufacture. Cigars were also made at Blackness by the Mitchell family, whose subsquent wealth built Glasgow's famous Mitchell Library, Europe's largest public source of reference.

Throughout the middle ages Blackness was Scotland's second most important seaport, only Leith further down river having more trade. Sailing ships were beached on the shore and their cargoes stored in the Guildry (the large thick stone-walled warehouse which the members of the Linlithgow trade guilds built at the shore end of the old pier). As the out port for that famous royal and ancient burgh, Blackness gained much trade from the import of goods for the royal court at Linlithgow Palace, ranging from fine clothes and tapestries to sturgeons and other fare for the lavish banquets often held there. To this day the shore at Blackness still forms the most easterly of the burgh boundaries and on the first Tuesday after the second Thursday in June when the ceremony of the Riding of the Marches takes places the Baron Baillie is still called upon to give his annual report on the life of the port and officially he still possesses the power to order the flogging of any drunk or disorderly sailors.

Proceeding down river from Blackness the next large harbour on the Lothian shore of the Forth is Port Edgar, which is now the main marina on the river. It takes its name from Edgar Ethling, the brother of Princess Margaret, who was with his sister when they were shipwrecked at this spot in 1069. During a severe gale the sailing boat on which they were trying to sail to the continent was blown off course and washed ashore.

Purchased by the Admiralty at the start of the First World War, Port Edgar became home to sixty-six destroyers and auxiliary vessels. In addition to their crews of 5,000 officers and sailors Port Edgar employed over 1,000 dockers at a time when Rosyth was still under construction. The boom ended in the 1920s partly because of the completion of Rosyth on the Fife shore opposite but also because of the growing post-war depression. In 1927 Port Edgar was put onto a care and maintenance basis. Its fortunes were revived with the outbreak of the Second World War when, as HMS *Lochinvar*, it became the navy's only mine sweeping training school, as this memorial stone bears testimony. Port Edgar was also the centre for the trial of all new mine disposal equipment. Butlaw Camp was hurriedly re-opened to provide additional barracks and the nearby naval hospital was also brought back into service.

Many boating enthusiasts now keep their craft at Port Edgar and this former Leith fishing boat was overhauled and restored there. The pictured vessel is named *Christina*.

Port Edgar is also home port to the Forth Conservancy Board's vessel, *Rover*.

The 'Burry Man', one of the strangest figures in British folklore, may owe his origins to the shipwreck of Prince Edgar and Princess Margaret. Local legend says he was originally a sailor washed up naked on the shores of the Forth, who clad himself in the green fruits of the burdock plant to protect his modesty before venturing into Queensferry to seek help. Another local tradition is that the Burry Man is a coastal variation of the Green Man. This second version of the Burry Man gains credence from the fact that his yearly visitation was said to guarantee good catches for the local fishing fleet when it set sail from Queensferry Harbour. The theory that he is indeed a fertility figure is supported futher by the floral bonnet which he always wears and by the colourful staffs of flowers which help him complete his rounds during which he has the right to demand a nip of whisky at every home he visits and a kiss from every bonnie lassie he encounters en route.

The Burry Man walks the streets of Queensferry every year from early morning until 5 p.m. in the evening on the Friday before Ferry Fair Saturday in mid-August.

Right: The Royal and Ancient Burgh of Queensferry takes its name from Queen Margaret, the princess who after being shipwrecked at Port Edgar sought refuge at the Scottish court and made the first crossing of the famous Queensferry Passage in order to reach it at Dunfermline. Once there she swiftly won the heart of the Scottish monarch, King Malcolm, who, although married at the time, soon divorced in order to marry her. The strong-willed Margaret also persuaded the Scottish king to abandon his Celtic faith and become a Roman Catholic. Keen to also convert the people of Scotland, Margaret established a free ferry to help persuade them to visit the shrines which she established at Dunfermline and St Andrews. Manned originally by the monks of Dunfermline Abbey, the ferry became the busiest sea route in Scotland. It was decided in 1794 in an attempt to improve the service that the rights to operate the ferry should be put up for annual auction. The result however was that the boatmen who won the rights were more anxious to make as much as possible during the next twelve months than to provide a good reliable service. Passengers complained that the piers, especially the one at the New Halls Inn, which became known as the Hawes, were in a ruinous and highly dangerous condition and that the ferrymen would often spend the fares on refreshments at the inn and were drunk and in an unfit state to man their boats. Especially annoying for travellers in a hurry was the fact that there were often no boats available on the Lothian side as most of the ferrymen had their homes in North Queensferry.

64

This view shows the Queensfery shore from which the ferry plied. As a result of all of their complaints in 1809, an Act of Parliament was passed to govern the operation of the Queensferry Passage and from then on it was very well run with two superintendents in charge. It was also laid down that the ferrymen were exempt from service in the Royal Navy and that soldiers in uniform were entitled to free passage. This privilege was also extended to licensed beggars, while for other travellers a table of fares was published. To hire a small boat during daylight hours cost half a crown, but if a traveller wished to cross after dark the cost doubled. Most importantly the Act laid down that ferries must be available at all hours and that at no time must more than two thirds of the vessels be at either side of the river. The next major change on the Queensferry Passage took place in 1821 when steam power was introduced for the first time on the crossing. The first steam ferry was very appropriately called *Queen Margaret*. She cost £2,369 and cost £12 0s 14p to operate each week, including fuel and the wages of the crew. Not only did she cut the crossing time to only twenty minutes but, when the wind fell, she was also capable of towing the other sailing boats engaged in the service.

South Queensferry. Albany Series

Two small boys survey the famous Queensferry Passage. Queen Victoria and Prince Albert made the crossing in 1842 while on their way north to enjoy a holiday in the Highlands. By this time the *Queen Margaret* had been replaced by what was decribed as, 'a very superior seaboat', the *William Adam*. She was 98ft in length with a beam of 32ft and sailed from the south side every hour and from North Queensferry on the half hour throughout the day. A contemporary account of Queen Victoria's crossing states, 'The day was most beautiful and the sea was covered by numerous steamers and other boats all gaily adorned. The whole scene was calculated to make a great impression not soon to be forgotten. It is understood the Sovereign expressed the greatest satisfaction with all of the arrangements made on board the steamer. Mr Mason the superintendent took the helm, while the attentive skipper Charles Roxburgh attended to the other duties.'

Port Edgar & South Queensferry

Right: The railway reached Dalmeny Station (top-right) in 1866, twenty-four years before the completion of the famous Forth Railway Bridge made it possible to continue its journey across the river. During the quarter century while trains had to terminate at Dalmeny, uniformed porters were provided to carry passengers' luggage up and down the steep flight of steps, known as Jacob's Ladder, to and from the ferries. This arrangement was always looked upon as very much second best to a much more ambitious scheme to build a branch line to Port Edgar from where it was planned to operate a train ferry across the Forth to Fife. This plan was delayed while arguments took place over an even more ambitious one to build a rail bridge to carry trains across the river between Blackness on the south shore and Charleston. In the meantime the operation of the ferry was taken over by John Croall, owner of the Antiquary, the last stage coach to maintain a regular service in Scotland. The ferry carried the coach on its daily run to and from Edinburgh and Dunfermline until Croall's death in 1873 brought a halt to its operation. The rights to the ferry were then purchased by the North British Railway which, in 1877, introduced the new ferry, named *John Beaumont* after one of its directors. Her engines proved inadequate to cope with the currents and tides on the crossing and two years later she was replaced by the *Thane of Fife* which was transferred from her existing duties on the railway company's service further down the Firth between Granton and Burntisland.

Total Length - - - - 1¾ miles | Deepest Foundation below High Water 91 ft.
Height from High Water - - 361 ft. | Weight of Steel - - - 51,000 tons
Clear Headway at High Water - 150 ft. | Total Cost - - - - £3,000,000

RELIANCE SERIES

The opening of the Forth Bridge in March 1890 greatly reduced demand for the ferry but the railway company still had an obligation to maintain a minimum service. This it did by providing a small subsidy to local captain John Arthur and later to Bo'ness tug boat owner John Wilson to provide a vessel.

View Showing Edinburgh Road and The Forth, South Queensferry

The arrival of the new-fangled petrol-driven motor cars brought an increase in business on the Queensferry Passage and trade increased still further during the First World War. John Wilson died shortly afterwards and, failing to lease the crossing to anyone else, the railway company found itself saddled with the route and it transferred the ferry *Dundee*, shown here, from the Tay. Already forty-five years old when she arrived in the Forth, the *Dundee* toiled to cope with the increase in traffic. Complaints mounted, but the railway was reluctant to invest during the economic depression. Then the far-sighted Clyde shipbuilder Maurice Denny agreed to operate the route and built two new vessels for it in order to keep the workforce at his Dumbarton yard employed.

Free to build the new ferries to his own design, Denny retained side loading as it allowed vehicles to be loaded at any state of the tide. More surprisingly he also decided to keep paddle power, but his pioneering electric paddle system was more efficient and gave the vessels greater ability to manoeuvre. Also revolutionary was the hull design, which created bows at both ends, and car decks entirely clear of obstruction apart from two small cabins at either end, one for shelter for foot passengers and the other with accommodation for the crew. Their central overhead bridge wheelhouses were designed to provide sufficient clearance for even the tallest furniture van. Denny also experimented with the new electric welding process on one ferry. The *Queen Margaret* was constructed using tradition rivets, while her sister ship, *Robert the Bruce* was built using electrical welding so that the yard could study the benefits of the new system.

Both *Queen Margaret* and *Robert the Bruce* were launched at a joint ceremony in 1934 and as soon as they arrived they introduced a thirty minute service, the first time that this had been achieved on the route since the 1840s. The service was soon interrupted as *Queen Margaret* had to be withdrawn to undergo minor repairs at Grangemouth's Carron Dry Dock. Soon after she returned the service was disrupted when *Robert the Bruce* ran aground off the Hawes Pier. She was not badly damaged and from then on the distinctive pair maintained an excellent service right through the remainder of the 1930s and on through the war years. Together they maintained the route until 1949 when Maurice Denny took a gamble that the plans to construct a new Forth Road Bridge would be sufficiently long delayed to justify building a third vessel. The *Mary Queen of Scots* was delivered to improve the service for which demand was growing steadily thanks to the relaxation of war time petrol rationing. *Mary Queen of Scots* was built to almost exactly the original plans.

Even with the frequent service provided by the ferries, two of which are seen in this photo, they couldn't cope with demand. In the early 1950s Sir Maurice, as he became, decided that it would be worthwhile to construct another ferry for the route. Keeping to the tradition he had established of naming the vessels of his fleet after famous Scots, this ferry was christened, *Sir William Wallace*. Although similar in appearance she was slightly larger and this, together with improvements to the piers on either side of the Forth, allowed for an improved fifteen minute schedule to be operated at peak times. Even with this faster turnaround, however, two hour waits were not uncommon and Sir Maurice had ambitious plans for a new super ferry, but the commencement of construction on the new Forth Road Bridge in 1958 meant that work never proceeded beyond the drawing board.

The building of the Forth Road Bridge began in 1958. Here work is seen proceeding on the southern approaches at Queensferry. (John Doherty)

Six years later, on Friday 4 September 1964, the Forth Road Bridge was officially opened on a foggy, grey morning by Her Majesty Queen Elizabeth. As Her Majesty and the Duke of Edinburgh drove north across the new bridge the sun broke through the mist. Once in Fife the royal car conveyed the Queen and Prince Philip to the pier at North Queensferry from which they sailed back aboard. *Queen Margaret* appropriately had the honour of making the last crossing on the nine-century old passage. In this photograph the road bridge is seen under construction with one of the Forth ferries which it was to replace seen far below. (John Doherty)

Crowds flocked to walk across the new Forth Road Bridge on its opening weekend in September 1964.
(John Doherty)

Queensferry's tiny harbour is now filled with pleasure craft, but in the nineteenth century it was home to the local fishing fleet and much of the town's revenue came from the tax levied on each barrel of salted herring exported mainly to the Scandinavian countries. Every year the Ferry fishermen used to declare, 'they'll be up to pay the rent,' meaning that the little gleaming sprats, or 'garvies', would swim up the Forth in their thousands every November. Not everyone welcomed the annual influx of fish because, as well as paying the rents, they also allegedly provided too much money for drink. The minister deplored the effect alcohol had on the morals of his congregation.

Resting on the oars allowed these local lads a beautiful view of their hometown. The long, low, single storey, white building overlooking the shore housed the famous Nardini's cafe, where the well-known local Italian family did a roaring trade serving ice cream in summer and fish and chip suppers on colder winter evenings. The three-storey building to the left was originally the most prestigious of the town's hotels, but later became the municipal chambers and during the Second World War was requisitioned and became the headquarters for the Free Norwegian Navy. Amongst the officers who spent the war years in exile here was Crown Prince Olaf. Every year in December the famous Shetland Bus – the unofficial ferry service which spanned the North Sea during the years of the hostilities – ensured that His Royal Highness received a little Christmas tree from his homeland.

Above: A ferry service still operates regularly from the historic Hawes Pier but it is strictly to provide transport for the men who work round-the-clock in shifts on Hound Point Terminal. The service is maintained by the sturdy little *Smit Young*. (Arthur Down)

Right: The Hawes Pier was designed by Robert Rennie and the little stone-built lighthouse at its landward end was the work of Robert Stevenson. The effects of weathering caused by the prevailing west wind are taking their toll on the sandstone of this fine little building. (Arthur Down)

After the closing of the ferry passage, Denny of Dumbarton tried to maintain a presence on the Forth by moving their small motor vessel the *Second Snark* to the Forth and operating summer sailings to allow passngers to view the newly-completed Forth Road Bridge. Unfortunately Scottish tourism in the 1960s was not sufficiently advanced to ensure the success of this venture and for over ten years there were no passenger sailings on the river. In the 1980s, however, local skipper John Watson purchased the motor vessel pictured here and undertook sailings down river to the island of Inchcolm. This picture show the vessel with which the service was inaugurated.

Demand for summer sailings on the Forth has grown steadily and now the route from Hawes Pier to Inchcolm is served by the *Maid of the Forth*. After a gap of twenty years, the *Maid* has now re-established Forth passenger sailings. Built in 1989 by David Abels of Bristol, she is the second vessel to bear the name and is now in her ninth year of operation. She is powered by two Ford Mermaid engines producing 120hp each and has a top speed of 9 knots with a cruising speed of 7 knots. Her 5,700 litre fuel capacity gives her an amazing range of 2,000 miles. The 130 ton *Maid* is equipped with hydraulic steering and as well as VHF radio, radar and echo sounder has the latest Global Positioning System, which tracks up to five satellites simultaneously so that she can track her position to within fifty metres anywhere in the world. The *Maid*, under her skipper, Captain Colin Aston, and her crew which often includes his daughters, Claire and Stephanie, working as Jills of all trades, usually stays much closer to home.

Third!

Inchcolm, to which the *Maid* provides a daily service throughout the summer months, is known as the 'Jewel of the Forth' or the 'Iona of the East' because of its historic Abbey.

The Abbey on Inchcolm is cared for by Historic Scotland and is open to visitors. Maid of the Forth is seen alongside the stone jetty.

As well as the regular sailings throughout the summer season by the *Maid of the Forth*, the river is also attracting increasing numbers of visits from much larger passenger vessels in the shape of luxury liners. Here the world's most famous passenger ship, *Queen Elizabeth 2*, is seen anchored off the Forth Bridge on a one day visit to the river in 2000.

Earlier the same year the famous Cunarder paid her longest ever visit to Scottish waters since she was launched from the yard of John Brown on the Clyde in September 1967, when she anchored off Anstruther for five days. Here she acted as a luxury floating hotel for golf enthusiasts attending the British Open at St Andrews.

At 70,000 tons and with a draught of 32ft, QE2 is too large to dock at Leith and the impressive height of her masts and funnel make it impossible for her to sail beneath the Forth Bridge (the bridge allows a maximum clearance of 150ft at low tide). Visits to the Forth therefore involve a tendering operation using both her own boats and local vessels including the *Maid of the Forth*. Here the *Queen* is seen from water level as one of her lifeboats transports passengers ashore.

Queensferry's famous Hawes Pier can be used at all states of the tide, making it an ideal place for QE2 to land her 1,800 passengers during her visits to the Forth. Passengers are also intrigued to learn of the pier's history in both fact and fiction and often stop to enjoy a drink in the white-harled, grey slate-roofed Hawes Inn, where popular Scottish author Robert Louis Stevenson set the scene of the actual abduction of his hero, David Balfour, in his most famous Scottish adventure novel, *Kidnapped*. Stevenson was very familiar with the Hawes because his family's firm built the little lighthouse on the pier for the Commissioners of Northern Lights.

During her first ever visit to the Forth in 1990 to mark the 150th anniversary of the founding of Cunard Line, arrangements were made to berth QE2 alongside the Hound Point Oil Terminal off the south shore of the Forth at Dalmeny. Normally, however, the terminal situated just down river from the Forth Bridge is home each day to two of the world's largest oil tankers, which dock there to export North Sea oil for the spot market at Rotterdam. The crude oil is pumped through a 500 mile long pipeline to Grangemouth. After processing there it is again sent by pipeline down river to Dalmeny where it is stored in tanks hidden from view in the heart of an old shale bing, until tankers of up to 300,000 tons each are ready to receive it at Hound Point Terminal.

BP employs three powerful tugs to ensure the safe berthing of the tankers. The tugs are all of similar design to the appropriately named *Dalmeny*, with a bollard-pulling power of over 100 tons. All possess fire-fighting ability. The newest of the tugs, the *Hopetoun*, joined the fleet in 1997 and was christened by the Marquis of Linlithgow, after whose stately home she takes her name. In addition to the three tugs, a small vessel maintains a ferry service to the terminal to transport the Berthing Master and his crew. Two smaller vessels are also on 24 hour standby to fight any possible oil spillage.

The suddenness and unexpectedness of how a collision may happen was illustrated in the Firth of Forth during the final days of the First World War. By this time many of the Royal Navy's North Sea Fleet were already laid up in Burntisland Bay. including the fleet's most unusual vessel, one of the world's first aircraft carriers, HMS *Campania*, which had three years earlier in 1915 been converted from the famous Cunard liner and former Atlantic Blue Riband holder of the same name. The 12,950 ton *Campania* was Clyde-built by Fairfields of Govan. Like all Cunard liners of the period her name ended in the letters, 'ia' and together with her sister ship, *Lucania*, also built by Fairfields, she was to revolutionise transatlantic travel, both because of her speed and her luxurious fittings which were unsurpassed in her period. Following *Campania*'s launch on 8 September 1892, however, Cunard were not happy with their new vessel because speed trials off the Isle of Arran revealed excessive vibration. *Campania* was Cunard's first twin screw vessel and the two huge German-designed propellers were deemed the source of the problem. Cunard threatened to sue Fairfields, but after the pitch of the propeller blades was changed the vibration was reduced. After seven months delay, *Campania* entered service on 22 April 1893. By the time she sailed on her maiden voyage the shaking was really only experienced by the 1,000 emigrates huddled together just as on the later White Star liner *Titanic* in steerage class. Meanwhile her 600 pampered guests in first class and 400 passengers in the almost equally comfortable second class accommodation, situated for'ard and amidships, never noticed the problem even when *Campania*'s captain ordered her full cruising speed of 22 knots. As they disembarked in the United States they were so full of praise for the delightfully comfortable crossing, which they had so much enjoyed, that on the return east bound trip, her master was encouraged to urge an extra knot from *Campania*'s two 15,000hp, triple expansion steam engines. She set a transatlantic record time of five days, seventeen hours and twenty seven minutes to win the fabled Blue Riband.

   Campania was the pride of the Cunard fleet and company literature boasted of her two enormous red funnels, each almost 20ft in diameter and rising an impressive 130ft from keel to rim to ensure power, and of her elegant and perfectly designed razor-sharp bow to ensure speed and her twenty lifeboats to ensure safety. Along with *Lucania*, which entered service later the same year, *Campania* put Cunard well ahead of all of its British and Continental rivals on the North Atlantic route. Throughout the first decade of the new century, *Campania* was the race horse of the Atlantic fleet, but by 1910 Cunard were becoming concerned about the expense of operating her. From her launch, *Campania*'s one hundred furnaces required to heat her thirteen boilers, ate up twenty tons of coal an hour, a huge five hundred tons of coal every day she was at sea and, as her engines grew older, they were becoming ever more expensive to fuel.

   Cunard therefore decided in 1914 to scrap *Campania*. The outbreak of war rescued her from the breakers because the Admiralty decided that with her length and speed she was the ideal vessel to convert into an aircraft carrier. With Britain at war, the cost of the coal and the wages of the 180 firemen and stokers required to achieve her speed no longer mattered! Until the outbreak of war, the efforts to utilise the newly available air power in naval warfare had depended on seaplanes, which both took off and landed on water, but now the Lords of the Admiralty were determined to gain the advantage of launching planes from ships and for that to succeed the speed of the vessel was all important. After *Campania* was purchased by the Royal Navy on 27 November 1914 she took almost eight months to refit, complete with a 168ft long wooden flight deck stretching all the way from her bridge to her bows. On 8 August 1915 the first trial of a ship-borne take off took place with *Campania* sailing straight into the wind at her maximum 23 knots. As the now twenty-three-year-old former liner surged forward, the pilot of the Sopwith Baby seaplane on her flight deck throttled back and thundered along the planks of the runway to make a successful take-off. He circled *Campania* and dipped his wings in salute before touching down in the water on the new aircraft carrier's lee side. The Sopwith was then hoisted safely back on board. Despite this success, it was decided that *Campania*'s flight deck was too short for operational use and so she was ordered back to port for further modifications to provide the additional length required. Her forward funnel was replaced with two narrow smoke pipes on either side of the now extended 200ft long runway and at the end of April 1916 *Campania* was ordered to rejoin the Grand Fleet at Scapa Flow.

It was then that *Campania*'s luck began to run out. Despite the long, light, Orcadian twilight at the end of May, her captain missed the signal to set sail to challenge the German Navy at Jutland. In the brief darkness of the northern night he further failed to see that the rest of the British Fleet had set sail from Scapa Flow. By the time dawn broke about two hours later and the mistake became obvious, the fleet was over forty miles out into the North Sea. *Campania* set to sea and, with her superior speed, would have caught up with them in time to play her part in the vital battle. Admiral Jellicoe doubted that she could arrive in time and ordered her back to Scapa Flow, thus robbing the Royal Navy of air reconnaissance in the ensuing fray. Her ill luck continued, when in August, repairs prevented her taking part in the next abortive attack on the German fleet. Despite these set backs, in 1917 *Campania* was equipped with specially-built two seat Fairey F 16s. They proved very successful as spotter planes and were named 'Campanias' after her. For the rest of the war, *Campania* was only kept at sea with difficulty because of problems with her engines and when, in October 1918, she anchored in the Forth off Burntisland with the rest of the Grand Fleet, it was decided she had little part left to play in the hostilities. Her complement was reduced from 374 to a skeleton maintenance crew. They alone were aboard on 5 November 1918 when the weather suddenly began to change. With only one of her thirteen boilers operational to provide auxiliary power, they could do little as the wind from the south west steadily increased to gale force.

Opposite, top: As the full force of the gale caught *Campania*'s long hull, she dragged her anchor and was swept astern. With her crewmen looking on helplessly, she collided amidships with the battleship, HMS *Royal Oak*. The tremendous impact caused *Campania*'s one operational boiler to explode with a bang which shook the whole of Burntisland. As local people rushed to the shore to see what had happened, they saw that *Campania* was sinking, but before she did the gale whipped her into another collision this time with the cruiser, HMS *Glorious*. The latter survived and ironically, after the end of the war was converted into an aircraft carrier to replace *Campania*.

Opposite, below: After ramming *Glorious*, some reports say that *Campania* continued out of control to collide with another battleship, HMS *Revenge*, but this is not confirmed and in any case she was by then so badly damaged that she began to go down. As she sank lower stern first into the waters of the Forth, all of her maintenance crew were rescued. Soon only her grey-painted funnel and the two grey smoke stacks, which had replaced her other forward funnel, remained sticking out of the water. All this was an embarrassment to the Royal Navy and it soon used the fact that her funnel and her smoke stacks were a hazard to shipping, entering and leaving the docks, to blow them up as part of an exercise. According to Admiralty charts *Campania*'s long hull lies broken in two on the bed of the Forth, but according to Colin Aston, master of *Maid of the Forth*, who is a keen diver, although her decks have collapsed, the long hull of the once proud Blue Riband holder is still intact. There are several other wrecks as close to shore as Burntisland Bay. One of the most dramatic of these disasters involved no less a person than King James VI's son, the ill-fated King Charles who, with his entourage came to the burgh towards the end of his first and only royal tour of Scotland in 1617, to board a fleet of ferries to carry them across the Forth. With a wind whipping in from the south west, the ferrymen were reluctant to put out into the Firth, but Charles was anxious to return to the comforts of Holyrood Palace and demanded that they set sail. They did and His Majesty reached the safety of Leith, but one of the accompanying boats, the *Blessed*, carrying several of his courtiers and all of the gold and other gifts received at his Scottish Coronation at Scone, did not and sank out in Burntisland Bay, thus giving Scotland its own version of England's King Alfred's disastrous crossing of the Wash. There have been attempts to recover the royal treasure, but even the most recent high-tech bid in 1995 yielded nothing of value.

Norwegian-registered vessels engaged in North Sea oilfield support work berthed in Burntisland's spacious dock. In the past cargoes of red bauxite were landed for use in the local aluminium factory, while coal mined in Fife pits formed the main export. Shipbuilding also took place in Burntisland for over 400 years. The Burntisland Shipyard Co. won a fine reputation for its cargo vessels, built in its yard to the west of the Old Dock. During the Second World War the yard built several auxiliary aircraft carriers as Atlantic convoy escorts. As well as providing air cover to protect the other ships, they were ingeniously designed to carry cargoes of American grain. A cut-away model of one of these auxiliary carriers, the *Empire McKendrick*, is on display in the town's museum. The museum is also home to the builder's model of the cargo vessel, *Maltese Prince*, which the yard launched for the Prince Line of London.

Milestones along Fife roads still remind drivers that distances were once calculated from Pettycur, situated on the coast between Burntisland and Kinghorn. From here a ferry originally plied across the Firth to Leith. Although Pettycur was a comparatively sheltered harbour, the crossing was often rough and as roads improved travellers preferred to go to Burntisland from where the crossing to Granton was more sheltered. Ferry operations at Pettycur ceased in 1848. One traveller who felt the full fury of a night crossing was King Alexander III. On a wild and windy March day in 1285 business in Edinburgh forced him to linger late, but he was determined to return home to his beautiful Spanish bride, Yolette, at Kinghorn Tower in Fife. Despite the gale Alexander succeeded in reaching the Fife shore, but he never reached Yolette because, as he rode along the cliff top above Pettycur, his horse missed its footing and he fell to his death. In the nineteenth century Pettycur regained some of its importance as a harbour when its golden sands resulted in a glassworks being established. Coastal steamers used to dock there to transport the bottles it produced.

The port of Kirkcaldy seen in this postcard view is now officially closed following damage several years ago to its dock gates, which proved too costly to repair.

Kirkcaldy New Harbour Works.

Kirkcaldy harbour at the east end of the town's long seafront esplanade is being redeveloped as a prime shopping and lesiure attraction. In its day the dock at Kirkcaldy had a considerable trade with imports and exports connected with the production of linoleum. This process created a distinct odour and it was often claimed that visitors smelled Kirkcaldy before they ever saw it.

THE

PROBLEM;

ITS ORIGIN AND DEVELOPMENT,

WITH A BRIEF SKETCH OF

THE LIFE OF THE INVENTOR,

DURING A THIRTEEN YEARS' RESIDENCE IN INDIA AND CHINA.

THE PROBLEM.

PRINTED FOR THE AUTHOR BY
W. G. BLACKIE AND CO., GLASGOW.
MDCCCXLIII.

by H. Dempster

see p. 72

Kirkcaldy was at one time also a shipbuilding town and this engraving shows the most unusual vessel built there. Designed by Henry Dempster, she was rather unwisely named *The Problem*. Described by her inventor as, 'a small triangular keel yacht' the 18ft vessel was launched from the yard of J. Brown & Co. in 1842. Her unusual appearance earned her the nickname of the 'Cockit Hat'. Dempster was convinced her unusual shape and rigging made her more maneuverable than conventional sailing vessels and set sail for London to try to persuade the Lords of the Admiralty. After visiting Dunbar, Eyemouth and Berwick-on-Tweed, she was damaged and abandoned in the Tyne. Undeterred, Dempster went on to produce his own design for well-decked fishing boats which would have allowed their catches to be kept alive until they reached market. He also invented a new trawl net which in 1868 was put on show at Calder's Sailmakers, Leith. Sadly, none of his work earned him any money. He died in North Leith Poor House in 1876 and lies buried in Rosebank Cemetery. (William Johnston)

Three
Leith and Granton

Granton was a bold Victorian enterprise started by the Duke of Buccleugh who owned the site at Wardie to the west of Edinburgh. He hoped to capitalise on the difficulties which ships were at that time experiencing in entering the well-established port of Leith at all times except high tide. Work was far enough advanced for Granton to be partially officially opened on 28 June 1838, the day of Queen Victoria's coronation. Seven years later its impressive pier, built entirely of stone from Granton Sea Quarry, was completed and work then began on the even longer East and West Breakwaters which stretched 3,170ft and 3,100ft out into the Forth. As there was a depth of 30ft of water at the entrance, ships could sail safely in and out at all states of the tide.

The Statistical Account of 1846 states that Granton provided '10 jetties, 2 low water slips, 11 warehouses and 10 cranes.' The enterprise of the Granton port authorities led to the North British Railway choosing it in 1848 as the southern terminal for the world's first rail ferries. Sir Thomas Bouch (who became infamous because of the disastrous collapse of his Tay Bridge) created an ingenious scheme of moveable stages and powerful stationary steam engines so that fully laden wagons and passenger carriages could be loaded and unloaded onto ferries at all states of the tide. The rail ferries were discontinued in 1890 when the completion of the Forth Rail Bridge made them redundant, but passenger and car ferries continued to operate the route until 1940. The service was resumed in March 1951 using ex-naval tank landing craft, named *Flora MacDonald*, *Bonnie Prince Charlie*, and *Thane of Fife*. Despite their romantic names, their flat bottoms and shallow draft provided an uncomfortable ride and they proved unsuccessful. The most recent attempt to run a ferry service across the Firth from Granton came in 1991 when Forth Ferries advertised a, 'fast passenger catamaran', *Spirit of Fife*, but it failed and was withdrawn after only one year.

The West Pier, Leith.

In Victorian times and on into Edwardian days, passenger sailings were, however, popular on the Firth as this postcard view of the West Pier at Leith shows. The paddle steamers were operated by the Galloway Steam Packet Co. Founded by Captain John Galloway around 1850 it at first offered pleasure sailings aboard two small former tug boats, but by the time his son, Mr X P. Galloway took control, it had what were described as, 'Five fine saloon steamers. These fast and commodious steamers of handsome appointment sail at stated times to many of the most historic and interesting riverside and coastal towns.

West Pier, Leith.

The passenger steamers which sailed from the West Pier were popular with Edinburgh city businessmen as their regular dependable sailings to seaside resorts such as Elie on the Fife shore allowed them to holiday with their wives and families and yet return to their desks each weekday.

Right: This poster advertised daily Forth steamer sailings from Leith to Aberdour. (William Johnstone)

Below: The *Fair Maid* was one of the most popular pleasure steamers on the Forth. Built by McKnight's of Ayr she was launched in 1866 and named *Madge Wildfire* after one of Sir Walter Scott's heroines. She was already over forty years old when she was bought by the Forth Towing Co. During the First World War she was requisitioned by the Admiralty but survived and returned to peacetime duties including Sunday School charters to Kinghorn and Aberdour. Following a second spell of war duties from 1939 to 1945 she made her final voyage back to the Clyde where she was broken up at Troon in 1947.

STEAM BETWEEN

LEITH, ABERDOUR

AND

INVERKEITHING

DAILY PLEASURE EXCURSIONS

THE FINE NEW STEAMER

CARRS

Plies DAILY between the above-mentioned Places as undernoted :—

LEITH HOURS

From LEITH New Pier to ABERDOUR and INVERKEITHING (or ST DAVID'S,) at 6·30 a.m., 10·30 a.m., and 4·30 p.m.

INVERKEITHING (or St DAVID'S) HOURS

From INVERKEITHING (or ST DAVID'S) to ABERDOUR and LEITH, at 7·30 a.m., 12·30 p.m., and 6·15 p.m.

ABERDOUR HOURS

From ABERDOUR to LEITH at 8·30 a.m., 1 p.m., and 7 p.m.

Passengers by first Boat in the morning from Inverkeithing and Aberdour will be in time for the Kirkaldy Boat at 9·30 from Leith.

FARES—Cabin 1s ; Steerage 9d.

N.B.—MR BLAIK, the Company's Agent at ABERDOUR, has safe Boats always in readiness to accommodate Parties wishing to visit the beautiful Island of INCHCOLME.

EXCHANGE BUILDINGS, LEITH,
1st August 1854.

The decks of the *Fair Maid* were crowded when this view was taken aboard her during an evening excursion sailing. There was often dancing on board on these occasions, but in this picture the only musician to be seen is a lone piper.

Despite the crowds on deck couples still found room to enjoy a dance on one of the *Fair Maid*'s popular evening excursion sailings down the Firth of Forth.

Leith Docks are seen from the air in this photograph taken during the 1960s looking from the east over the Western Harbour, which is now dominated by the Ocean Terminal and where the former Royal Yacht *Britannia* is permanently berthed.

The piers of Newhaven Harbour, where the fishmarket used to be, house the popular heritage museum and Harry Ramsden's Fish Restaurant. The Water of Leith is seen flowing from left to right across the middle of the picture and is a reminder that Leith was originally simply a tidal harbour where this tributary flowed into the Forth. Leith expanded as a port after the magistrates employed eminent civil engineer Robert Rennie in 1799 to design enlarged piers and wet docks which ran parallel to Commercial Street. Work on digging the dock began in 1800 at a cost of £160,000 and was completed in 1806. The neighbouring West Dock, sometimes called the Queen's Dock, was begun in 1810 and opened in 1817. Together these two docks covered an area of 10¼ acres and could accommodate around one hundred and fifty small sailing vessels. Rennie's ambitious scheme also included three graving docks and several drawbridges. The total cost was £285,000 plus a further £8,000 spent on a new bridge over the Water of Leith. (Forth Ports plc)

Above: The complex of Leith Docks is again seen from the air in this second 1960s photograph, this time from out over the Forth looking inland over the Trinity area of Edinburgh. Leith's innermost dock, the Edinburgh, located to the east of the Albert, to which it was linked by a broad channel, was officially opened in July 1881 by the Duke of Edinburgh. The total masonry needed to construct this $16\frac{1}{2}$ acre basin was 900,000 cubic feet, most being obtained from Craigleith Quarry. Since 1981 all grain cargoes discharged at Leith have been handled at the Imperial Dock. Three suction discharge towers can each handle 220 tons an hour. During the 1980s all of the equipment at the Imperial Dock was modernised and it now offers the best deep water berths in the east of Scotland.(Forth Ports plc)

Tall-masted sailing ships still dominated the view when this postcard photograph was taken towards the end of Queen Victoria's reign. In 1890 one hundred and eighty-one ships were registered at Leith. They included the thirty-strong fleet of the famous Currie Line whose vessels carried not only cargo but passengers. Passenger services included twice-weekly sailings to Hamburg, with weekly departures for Copenhagen, Kristiansand and Stetin and a once-a-fortnight voyage to Bremerhaven.

Another well-known Leith Line, George Gibson & Co. owned twelve steamers which maintained cargo and passenger sailings twice weekly to Rotterdam, once weekly to Dunkirk and once-a-fortnight to Amsterdam. In this picture postcard view a steamer is seen sailing out of Leith's Outer Harbour into the Firth of Forth.

Left: The swing bridge is seen in this view of Leith Harbour at the mouth of the Water of Leith. A riverside walk now flows the course of the Water of Leith all the way inland from the docks to Balerno. In March 2002 author Ian Rankine of Inspector Rebus fame launched the investigative trail which visitors can trace along its length. The Water of Leith Visitor Interpretation Centre at Slateford tells the story of this historic waterway which runs through the heart of the Scottish capital to reach the Firth at Leith. This stretch of the Water of Leith round the old harbour is now a fashionable restaurant area with many enticing eating places.

This view again shows the Outer Harbour and the entrance to the Port of Leith.

The full expanse of Leith's Imperial Dock is seen to advantage in this photograph.

Leith's Imperial Dock is seen from a different angle in this second postcard view with the Firth of Forth and the island of Inchkeith in the background.

The thirty-strong fleet of the famous Currie Line included the SS *Weimar*, which operated the company's twice-weekly service from Leith to Hamburg.

The port's most frequent passenger and cargo sailings were the thrice-weekly departures by the well-appointed steamers of the London & Edinburgh Steam Shipping Co. bound for the Thames. The company was founded in 1809 by a group of merchants from Edinburgh and Leith to improve the reliabilty of the sailings between the Scottish and English capitals. This they managed to do and the Union Company which had provided a service from Berwick on Tweed to London for the previous half century moved its headquarters also to Leith in order to compete, but in 1809 it was merged with the new Edinburgh line. Even after the two cities were linked by rail the London & Edinburgh Shipping Co.'s overnight voyages linking the capitals were still favoured by many travellers with steamers including the *Royal Archer* and the *Royal Scot* replacing the line's original sailing clippers. Travelling by sea to London remained a popular option until the outbreak of hostilities in 1914 dealt a heavy blow to the company. During the Second World War all of its vessels were lost. It acquired three new vessels but passenger sailings were not resumed. The company's last ship, the *Belvina*, was sent to the breakers yard in 1958 and the following year, after 150 years in business, this well known Leith firm finally closed.

Leith Nautical College was founded by John Lockie at 32, Sandport in 1880. Lockie was born in 1853 and died in 1919. Before coming to Leith he was assistant to Lord Kelvin at the Univeristy of Glasgow. Later he became assistant to Professor Archer at the University of Edinburgh. Before founding the Nautical College he also ran Lockie's Engineering Academy and the Leith Science College, of which he was the principal for fourteen years. The Nautical College eventually outgrew the buildings shown here in this photograph and moved to modern new premises on the eastern outskirts of the city. The new building was designed to look like an ocean liner complete with a mock funnel, bridge and wheelhouse. Facilities for the students included a rooftop planetarium. In the 1990s, however, the rationalisation of the education of officers for the mercantile marine resulted in all Scottish courses being transferred to Glasgow Nautical College on the south shore of the River Clyde. The Edinburgh building is still used as a technical college.

Above: This cargo steamer with her tall funnel dominated the dock scene when this photograph was taken probably in the early 1920s.

Left: A cargo steamer named *Britannia* lies berthed in this view of Leith Docks, a reminder that her much more famous namesake, the former royal yacht *Britannia*, has found a permanent berth nearby in the Western Harbour. The current *Britannia*, built at John Brown's, Clydebank, was launched in 1953 and served the royal family for forty-five years.

The *Liberty* was one of many fine yachts built by the Leith yard of Ramage & Ferguson. Ramage & Ferguson opened their premises in 1878 and became a registered company in 1892.

This photograph shows the launch of one of the yachts for whose construction Ramage & Ferguson became justly famous.

Another of the fine steam yachts built by Ramage & Ferguson is depicted in this view. In 1918 Ramage & Ferguson & Co. was taken over by Ellerman Lines. Three years later the Leith yard launched the most famous vessel ever built there, the magnificent five-masted *Kobenhavn* which it constructed for the East Asiatic Co. of Denmark. Tragically seven years later she was lost without trace off the coast of South West Africa.

This view shows another of the graceful yachts built by Ramage & Ferguson. Building for such an upmarket clientele meant that the Leith yard was badly affected by the Wall Street stock market crash of 1929 and the depression that followed it. Orders became hard to find and as a result the yard closed in 1933. The last vessel launched was the auxiliary barquentine *Mercator*, which was built as a training ship for the Belgian government. (See page 126)

what about Henry Robb – lasted much longer than Ramage & Ferguson!

East Coast Salvage Coy Limd. Leith

Directors

RICHARD RAMAGE. Esq. Shipbuilder. Chairman
CHRISTIAN SALVESEN. Esq. Shipowner xxxxx
HUGH ROSE Esq. Merchant ∞∞∞∞∞∞∞
T. NAPIER-ARMIT. Esq. Salvage Engineer

SECRETARY

FRANCIS F. REID Esq · Shipowner.

Telegraphic Address "ARMIT LEITH."

Offices ~ 24 BERNARD ST. LEITH.

Telephone No 584.

Richard Ramage was also chairman of the East Coast Salvage Co. whose other directors included the well-known Christian Salvesen, merchant Hugh Rose and salvage engineer T. Napier-Armit.

LIST OF WRECKED PROPERTY RECOVERED BY

❋ MR ARMIT. ❋

QUEEN OF THE BELGIANS, s.s., Launched 1869.
COURIER, s.s., Pumped out 1869.
MARSEILLES, Capsized in 1873.
FIONA, s.s., Sunk 1873.
ROSEBUD, s.s., Sunk 1874.
SEAWARD, Sunk 1874.
MARIA, D. C., Ashore 1875.
LOCH LAGGAN, Sunk 1875.
GEORGIAN, s.s., Sunk 1875.
COLUMBO, Sunk 1876.
THAMES, s.s., Sunk 1876.
MABEL, s.s., Sunk 1876.
PRINCESS BEATRICE, s.s., Sunk 1877.
NESTOR, s.s., Collision 1877.
LARNE, s.s., Capsized 1877.
ST CLAIR, s.s., Sunk 1877.
CAIRNGORM, Ashore 1877.
SEAL, s.s., Ashore 1878.
GROSSER KURFURST, Sunk 1879.
POMERANIA, s.s., Sunk 1879.

TAY BRIDGE WRECK, 1880.
CAROLINE, s.s., Sunk 1880.
SORATA, s.s., Sunk 1880–81.
IONA, s.s., Sunk 1882.
HELENSLEA, Sunk 1882.
VESUV, s.s., Sunk 1883.
DREDGER, Capsized 1883.
DAPHNE, s.s., Capsized 1883.
EMILY, s.s., Ashore 1883.
BARMORE, s.s., Sunk 1883.
LOCH NESS, s.s., Stranded 1883.
ATLANTA, Ashore 1884.
CAMOENS, s.s., Sunk 1884.
GLENCOE, s.s., Ashore 1884.
AUSTRIA, s.s., Sunk 1884.
ADAM SMITH, s.s., Capsized 1885.
CARTVALE, Sunk 1886.
CUXHAVEN, s.s., Sunk 1886.
DREDGER, Sunk 1886.
ASHURST, s.s., Stranded 1886.
COLE ROCK, Salved Cargo 1887.

WALTON, s.s., Sunk 1887.
EUREKA, s.s., Broken in two 1887.
GREATA, s.s., Stranded 1888.
MILAN, s.s., Ashore 1888.
RADNOR, s.s., Ashore 1888.
SALATIGA, Capsized 1888.
CUMBERLAND, s.s., Ashore 1888.
HECTOR, s.s., Sunk 1889.
CHARLES BALL, Sunk 1889.
JEHU, Stranded 1890.
SIMON DUMOIS, s.s., Stranded 1890.
BATTLEISLE, s.s., Sunk 1890.
GLEN GRANT, Stranded 1890.
ORION, s.s., Stranded 1890.
ST ROGNVALD, Stranded 1891.
UTOPIA, Sunk 1891.
SOPHIE, Stranded 1891.
KOPERNIKUS, Stranded 1891.
HOWARD, Sunk 1891.
FLORENCE, s.s., Stranded 1891.

The advertisement for the East Coast Salvage Co. Ltd proudly lists all of the wrecks recovered by its salvage engineer, T. Napier-Armit.

This further advertisement for the company lists some of the salvage appliances available at the company's store at the Old Dock.

The Leith-registered North of Scotland Steam Navigation Co.'s *St Rognvald*, which operated a weekly passenger and cargo service from its home port to Orkney and Shetland, was one of the vessels salvaged by the East Coast Salvage Co. Ltd. when she was stranded on rocks at Workhead, near Kirkwall, Orkney. The *St Rognvald* was refloated and towed south to Aberdeen.

Saints ran till 2002., But from Aberdeen

not even for Leith

No

The last of the Saints, MV *St Ninian*, which was the final ship to provide a passenger service from Leith to Lerwick, still survives. She is seen here berthed in Leith prior to her sale to Canadian owners and continues to operate in Nova Scotia. (Dr Louis Rusack)

Aboard MV *St Ninian* en route from Leith to Lerwick. *St Ninian* also called regularly at Aberdeen and Kirkwall in the Orkneys. Mini cruises aboard this attractive vessel were a popular attraction. This photograph was taken by a regular passenger on the *St Ninian* and the other vessels of the North of Scotland Steam Navigation Co.'s reliable fleet, Haddington GP, Dr Louis Rusack, who named one of his sons after *St Ninian*'s older sister ship, *St Rognvald*. (Dr Louis Rusack)

This is another of *St Ninian*'s older sisters in the North of Scotland Steam Navigation Co.'s fleet, *St Magnus*, berthed in Leith prior to one of her voyages to the Northern Isles. Dr Rusack's son, Ronnie, who is now skipper of the fleet of popular restaurant barges that sail on the Union Canal from the Edinburgh Canal Centre at Ratho, recalls travelling aboard *St Magnus* and watching fascinated as a herd of cattle was loaded for the voyage south from the islands. (Dr Louis Rusack)

The trim Danish-owned *Gulfoss*, with her black-painted hull and superstructure and her funnel with its two white bands, also operated a regular passenger service from Copenhagen to Leith and then north to Reykjavik, the capital of Iceland. (Dr Louis Rusack)

The 40,000 ton MV *New Prospect*, one of the largest cargo vessels ever to berth at Leith is seen here on 29 July 1991 discharging pipes for use in the North Sea oil industry. Notice the helicopter pad on the bows of the vessel seen beyond the two cargo sheds. (Forth Ports plc)

MS *Royal Viking Sun*, the largest passenger vessel ever to call at Leith, is seen here with her white-painted superstructure looming over the two tugs which guided her into the port in August 1994. The 37,845 ton *Sun* was later purchased by the Carnival-owned Seabourn Line and after completing her 2002 world cruise was, in April of that year, stretched by the addition of a new middle section of cabins. When she returned to service her owners Carnival transferred this famous five-star ship to operate under the flag of Holland America Line. Now too large to sail through the entrance lock into Leith docks, it is still hoped that she will return to Scotland, with Forth Ports plc making alternative arrangements for her to berth at Rosyth. (Forth Ports plc)

Four

The Firth of Forth
Muselburgh to Dunbar and Fife

The River Esk flows into the Forth at Musselburgh and because of this the town was originally known as Eskmouth. Its tidal harbour at Fisherrow was for many years a busy fishing harbour, but now is occupied by small pleasure craft.

Fisherrow, Morrison's Haven ?

A short distance further down the Lothian shore of the Firth, the two tall chimneys of Cockenzie Power Station, which now look over the former fishing village, are a well-known landmark for sailors on the river.

Nestling in the shadow of the massive coal-fired power station, little Cockenzie Harbour is still home to many small vessels, but pleasure craft now vastly outnumber the locally-owned fishing boats, which now mainly use the more modern facilities at neighbouring Port Seton.

This mosaic wall by the harbourside at Cockenzie was designed by the pupils of the town's primary school, under the guidance of well-known Scottish artist Kenny Munroe, as a tribute to their grandfathers who fished from the port. There now seems little prospect of Cockenzie ever becoming a major fishing port again as the industry is concentrated more and more on major centres such as Peterhead, Fraserburgh and at Eyemouth. This little port's most famous sailor was Captain Francis Cadell the youngest of four sons of the Cadell family of Cockenzie House. He joined the Royal Navy as a midshipman and, after fighting in the Opium Wars with China, rose to command his own vessel. He later opened the mighty Murray River in Australia to navigation, sailing its length in a collapsible, canvas, blunt-nosed canoe which he called Forerunner. A replica of Forerunner was built by artist Kenny Munroe and in 2002 he sailed it from near the source of the Forth at Aberfoyle down river to Cockenzie, while a similar reconstructed vessel set sail from Goolwa at the mouth of the Murray in South Australia as part of a joint venture between the two little ports to commemorate the 150th anniversary of the success of Captain Cadell.

Despite the tendency for the fishing fleet to move to larger harbours, neighbouring Port Seton still has some vessels based there and landings are still made. The little town's fish merchants have an excellent reputation for the excellence of their catch and visitors who come to Seton Sands Holiday Village still look forward to their fish suppers served by fish and chip shops around the old harbour as well as by a fish and chippy within the boundaries of the village.

Did Prestonpans have a harbour? Boat in register at A.N. Arbroath!

Prestonpans, to which this fishing boat belonged, took its name from the salt pans which flourished there until the end of the 1950s, producing coarse salt using locally produced coal to evaporate the water from the Forth. The salt produced provided the town's little harbour with a prosperous export trade as it was in great demand in the Low Countries and by Scandinavia.

These modern sculptures now top the sea wall at Preston Pans.

The thick stone-walled, red pantile-roofed granary and warehouse on the shores of the Firth at Aberlady has been converted into attractive apartments, but it is still a reminder of the centuries when its little tidal harbour was the bustling outport for the nearby inland burgh of Haddington.

This very traditional slate-roofed Scottish villa overlooking the bay at Aberlady with its sailing ship carved and painted above the front door is another reminder of the days in past centuries when the village harbour was used by vessels landing cargoes for the merchants of Haddington. The customs house, now known as Kilspindie House, still stands near the greens of the golf course. Despite the existence of the customs house, however, Aberlady is said in past centuries to have been the haunt of smugglers who had their headquarters in a narrow street called the Wynd. Aberlady is now a quiet, peaceful backwater, popular with holiday makers, who enjoy bird watching and exploring the nature reserve which has been established in Aberlady Bay.

Despite its difficult entrance from the Forth, North Berwick Harbour had a commercial trade exporting agricultural products and importing cargoes of coal and what was discreetly referred to in the harbour master's register as 'tons of guano.' This was the droppings of the thousands of gannets that nested on the nearby Bass Rock out in the Firth, which was sold as manure to the farmers of East Lothian.

North Berwick Harbour is now used almost exclusively as a safe haven by yachts and dinghies. It is also home to the MV *Sula II*, the wooden-hulled pleasure vessel which, during the summer season, carries visitors on trips around the Bass Rock and to the little island of Fidra where they are allowed ashore. Fidra is the site of the lighthouse built by the famous Stevenson family and it is claimed that it is the inspiration for Spy Glass Island in Robert Louis Stevenson's famous children's adventure story *Treasure Island*. This 1950s view of the harbour shows the original *Sula* (which took her name from the Latin name for the gannets which the visitors come to see on the Bass Rock) departing on one of her popular cruises.

Right: Robert Louis Stevenson spent several childhood summer holidays in North Berwick while his father was working on the construction of the new lighthouse on the island of Fidra.

Left: Stevenson always loved the sea and this was the vessel which he sailed in the Pacific. He chartered the schooner *Casco* in San Francisco from her owner, Dr Merritts, in June 1888. He ended his cruise at Honolulu in January 1889. Shortly afterwards the *Casco* was purchased by the Victoria Sealing Co. When sealing was banned by international agreement in 1912 the *Casco* was sold and was laid up in Vancouver Harbour until 1918 when she sailed back to her old home in San Franciso. During that year she took a cargo of lumber to Fiji and in June 1919 sailed for Siberia with a party of gold hunters. On the return voyage she was wrecked on King Island in Alaska.

North Berwick harbour gained a degree of notoriety at Hallowe'en 1589 when it was the scene of one of the best recorded alleged examples of witchcraft in Scottish history. Under cover of darkness a small armada of boats sailed down the Forth from Cockenzie. Its Admiral-in-Chief was the sinister black-cloaked Dr Sin, who was by day John Cunningham, the dominie at the school in that East Lothian burgh. On that pitch black night he was accompanied not by his scholars, but by ninety-four of their mothers who had fallen under his persuasive evil spell. That final night of the month of October he was, however, in a foul mood, angrier even than when in the classroom by day he regularly whipped their offspring with his thick, thonged, black leather tawse. For they had taken longer than he had anticipated to make the voyage down the coast from Cockenzie and now he was late for his appointment with Auld Nick, the Devil! Despite his exhortations to hurry, his women followers shouted, danced and capered their way noisily along the high sea wall at the harbour. Their shrieks and shouts were silenced the moment they entered North Berwick Parish Kirk, whose ancient ruins can still be seen at the harbourside, for there in the pulpit loomed the black-clad figure of Satan, 'with goat-like beard and flowing tail' as a contemporary account described him. It is now believed that the Devilish figure was no less a person than Francis Stewart, the Earl of Bothwell, in disguise, because the business of that night was to plot the murder of King James VI and his new, young, bride, Princess Anna of Denmark, as the royal couple sailed home to Scotland. Cunningham, alias Dr Sin, and his alleged coven of witches were subsequently arrested. While the women were let off with a warning, Cunningham was tried at a show trial at Edinburgh Castle, tortured with the thumbscrews which were used on him for the first time in Scotland and in the end executed by being burned at the stake on the Castle Hill. The place of his terrible death is marked to this day by the little witches' fountain at the foot of the Castle Esplanade.

'One wonderful crag rising within the sea,' is how fifteenth century writer, Hector Boece, described the Bass Rock in his *History and Chronicles of Scotland*. The gannet colony on the rock is the largest on the east coast of Britain. In this view taken from the south shore of the Firth the Bass is overlooked by the ruins of Tantallon Castle, whose massive, thick red stone curtain walls made it an impregnable fortress.

The lighthouse on the Bass was designed by the Stevenson family. It was completed in 1902 at a cost of £8,087 10s and a very exact 4d and its light first beamed out on 1 November of that year. The intensity of the light was described as 156 candelas. With its elevation 150ft above sea level its signal of six white flashes every half minute could be seen at a distance of twenty-one miles. For almost ninety years lighthouse keepers did month-long spells of duty on the Bass before enjoying two week breaks ashore at the keepers' cottages at Granton. Each day throughout their turn of duty the chief keeper and his assistant had to climb the spiral, newal, turnpike stairway to reach the top of the 67ft high whitewashed tower to clean the lamp, which was powered by paraffin produced by James Paraffin Young's mineral oil company in Midlothian.

This view shows boating off Dunbar. During the time of the Republican Commonwealth in the 1650s the Lord High Protector's government gave £300 to improve Dunbar harbour, which was from then on known as Cromwell's Harbour. It was, however, not until it was replaced in 1844 by the new Victoria Harbour that Dunbar really became important as a port. Compared to the old harbour, the new one had a safer entrance and was more spacious, large enough indeed to accommodate over three hundred fishing boats, when Dunbar was at its height as a herring port.

Dunbar is now a popular small holiday resort and shopping centre for the surrounding area and the harbour is still busy with small pleasure craft as seen in this photograph. (Dr Arthur Down)

The Barns Ness Lighthouse is also situated on the south coast of the Firth to the east of Dunbar. It looms over the little, white, harled houses where its keepers and their families used to have their homes before it was automated. The operation of its light, which can be seen for a distance of twenty-one nautical miles, is now controlled by computer from the headquarters of the Northern Commissioners of Lights in George Street, Edinburgh. (Dr Arthur Down)

Dysart's harbour, on the opposite Fife shore of the Firth, to the east of Kirkcaldy, used to have a flourishing commercial trade in both coal and salt and could accommodate vessels with a draught of up to 18ft. The harbour also used to export textiles ranging from fine linen, some of which was manufactured in the village's own mill, to woollens and tweeds produced in other Fife towns. Dysart is the birth place of John McDougal Stewart, who in 1861 became the first man to cross Australia from the south to the north. His home is now a museum. The village also has close links to famous Scottish author John Buchan, who spent childhood summer holidays there with his family. The opening scenes of his adventure *Prester John* are believed to have been influenced by his youthful memories of exploring the shore near Dysart. The village's quaint homes are protected under the National Trust for Scotland's Little Houses Scheme and of particular interest is Pan Ha' as its name is a reminder of the little port's links with the salt industry.

Buckhaven was, as its name suggests, at one time a harbour on the Fife shore of the Forth. It is often referred to by its inhabitants as Buckhind which is a reference to the deer in its title.

West Pier, Buckhaven Harbour

Hearty Greetings from Buckhaven

Buckhaven enjoyed a revival of its seafaring fortunes when it became a site for the construction of rigs for the North Sea oil fields.

West Wemyss, Leven ?

New Dock, Methil.

Methil remained an important East Coast port throughout both world wars, so much so that during the Second World War it attracted the attention of German spies, perhaps interested in the fact that all of Britain's North Sea convoys formed up just off its shore. Stories of Methil's 300-year history as a coal exporting port since the second Earl of Wemyss opened its first harbour in 1662 and of the Wellesley and the other pits which supplied it are brought to life in the Heritage Centre, which now occupies the 1930s post office building in Lower Methil's High Street.

114

The sterns of these old steamers are a striking featureof this old picture postcard view of the docks at Methil. Methil dock is still open and operated by Forth Ports Plc, but its trade now is only a fraction of the three million tons of coal which it exported each year at the beginning of the twentieth century, when it was the busiet coal port in Scotland.

This early picture postcard view captures well the charm of St Monance in the East Neuk of Fife. Neuk means a wee corner and St Monance is indeed tucked away but it has nevertheless a proud tradition of shipbuilding dating from 1747 when the Miller family founded their yard adjacent to the harbour. For eight generations James. N. Miller & Sons specialised in building all kinds of small craft from fishing boats to both sailing and motor yachts with occasional additional orders for pilot boats and Admiralty launches for the Royal Navy.

This second postcard photograph shows St Monance of past decades when the launching of a Miller-built boat was always a big occasion in the little Fife fishing port. For the launch of larger vessels built in the company's main shed to the east of the harbour a section of railway sleepers on the pier was lifted to provide direct access to the waters of the Firth. Smaller boats were built in the company's other premises in Shore Street, and Virgin Square was always packed with crowds to see them trundled out to be launched at the harbour, which has recently been converted into a marina for pleasure sailors.

Pittenweem is one of the most picturesque of the fishing villages on the Fife coast. It is still also a busy working harbour with a modern fish market on the quayside.

Pittenweem means the Place of the Cave and a cave can indeed be visited in Cove Wynd. The little cave is traditionally linked to seventh-century Saint Filian. The town has been a burgh since the reign of King James II and its market cross which bears the town's coat of arms is dated 1711. Pittenweem was the birthplace of the Henderson brothers who founded the Anchor Line whose liners took many Scottish emigrants to new lives in North America

Anstruther and Cellardyke were rival ports for centuries as each had its own fishing fleet. In the middle of Queen Victoria's reign, however, the Anstruther fishing fleet grew too large for its little harbour, and the Government was persuaded in 1866 to provide funds for the much larger Union Harbour seen in this photograph. Construction of it proved a very arduous task as frequent storms interrupted work and swept away what had already been achieved, but in the end in 1877 it was completed at a cost of £80,000. As it was constructed to the east of the old one in Shore Street, Easter Anstruther, its better facilities and sheltered waters, protected by a western breakwater and an eastern pier 1,200 yards long, proved sufficiently attractive to lure the Cellardayke fishermen to berth their boats there too. Although it covers an area of all of 13½ acres and was designed to cater for all of five hundred fishing boats, the new Union Harbour must often have been crowded, because the report of the Fishery Board for Scotland for 1883 states that the number of fishing craft of all classes belonging to the Anstruther District was 830.

Anstruther District was one of twenty-six areas into which the Scottish fishing industry was divided and it was the most prosperous with one in eight of the fishing fleet having it as their port of registration. These 830 boats employed 3,491 fishermen and boys, of whom 2,050 had their homes in the district. The fishing also provided almost as many jobs in ancillary industries with a further 2,362 men and women earning their living as fish curers and coopers. During the last century Anstruther's fishing fleet has mainly relocated to the harbour at Pittenweem.

Cellardyke has changed little since this picture postcard view of it was taken almost a century

This early picture postcard view again shows Cellardyke to advantage. With its beautiful views out across the Firth of Forth, it remains a very popular holiday village, although it is no longer a working fishing port.

Crail, St. Andra's.

Elie lighthouse is seen in this picture postcard view. Up until the outbreak of the First World War, paddle steamers used to berth alongside Apple Rock pier so that their passengers could enjoy a sedate walk ashore along the causeway for a brief visit to Elie. The causeway was built during the 1850s by William Baird to link what had, until that time, been a little tidal islet, known as the Elie of Ardross to the mainland. This made it easier to transport ashore the cargoes stored in the thick stone-walled four-storey-high granary building, which still dominates the harbour scene and acts as a reminder that Elie once had a commercial trade rather than just catering for water sports enthusiasts as it does now.

Right: The history of the Isle of May is also the history of its lighthouses. The first lighthouse on the May, which was one of the first around the shores of Scotland, was erected in 1635 by the then owner of the island, Alexander Cunninghame of Barnes. He had shortly before obtained a royal charter to the island from King Charles I during his one and only visit to Scotland in 1633. In partnership with James Maxwell of Innerwick, over on the mainland to the south of Dunbar, he constructed a three-storey tower with a brazier at the top. Each evening at dusk a fire was built and fed with coal to produce a light throughout the whole night. To keep it burning every night throughout the year, 380 tons of the stuff had to be ferried out to it annually and to pay for this a duty was imposed on all ships sailing through the waters between St Abbs Head to the south and Dunottar to the north. The light was not very effective, however, as in poor weather conditions when it was most needed, it was scarcely visible and, when gales blew up the Firth, the fire was often extinguished by the howling wind. There was particular discontent about the warning light on the May after the Union of the Parliaments in 1707 because, despite the fact that Great Britain was now officially one country, the island's owners still insisted on charging English and Irish vessels double dues, just as they did all other foreign vessels. The tax, however, on all shipping continued to be imposed until after the end of the Napoleonic Wars. Fifteen years earlier in 1800, it was let for as high a sum as £1,500. Despite the fact that the light was improved during this period by the simple method of burning more coal, it was not sufficient to save two of the Royal Navy's frigates, HMS *Nymphon* and HMS *Pallas*, which in 1810 ran aground on the south shore of the Firth near Dunbar. At the Court of Inquiry into their loss it was stated that the wrecks occurred because both captains were misled by the glow of the fire of a limekiln at Skate Row near Torness, on the East Lothian shore, which was glowing much more brightly and effectively than the official light out on the May.

Before the building of the lighthouses on the shores of the Forth, some unscrupulous inhabitants of the Forth coastal villages called 'the wreckers' used to try to lure vessels ashore by displaying lanterns near dangerous rocks and Robert Louis Stevenson devoted one of his short stories to their activities. There was also always a considerable amount of smuggling on the Forth. The Black Castle, whose building dates from 1626, in South Queensferry's High Street was alleged to be one of their headquarters with secret passages leading under the street to the shore so that they could land their contraband without being spotted and arrested.

RUINS OF
St ADRIANS
MONASTERY   NEW LIGHT HOUSE.
ISLE of MAY   3 MILLION CANDLE POWER
R.P. Phillimore   Isle of MAY. 58)   PILOTS OLD LIGHT
    SHELTER. HOUSE. 1636

The May lighthouse was afflicted by ill luck on several other occasions. Its first lighthouse keeper was drowned off the island in rough seas. His death was said to have been caused by witchcraft and, over on the mainland in Anstruther, a local woman called Effie Lang was arrested and ultimately charged with the crime. She was accused of using her black magic powers to raise the viciously violent storm, which resulted in the keeper's drowning. Although she had never in her life set foot on the Isle of May, she was in the end found guilty of the, 'horrid and abominable crime of witchcraft,' and ordered to pay the penalty for her dreadful deed. She was therefore duly executed by being put to death by being strangled, after which her body was burned at the stake. Later, towards the end of the eighteenth century, tragedy struck again. Passing ships reported that the light on the May was out and when this was investigated it was discovered that the keeper, his wife and their five young children all lay dead in their beds. They had died from carbon monoxide poisoning, having breathed in the fumes from the fire fueling the light; too many coal cinders had been allowed to build up, thus cutting off the ventilation. When the Barnes' family estate including the May was sold, the island was purchased by Scott of Scotstarvet in Fife. It was later inherited by General Scott, whose daughter, the Duchess of Portland, sold it in 1814 to the Commissioners of Northern Lighthouses for the amount of £60,000. Partly because of the wreck of the *Nymphon* and the *Pallas*, which it was reckoned had cost the Government £100,000, an Act of Parliament was quickly passed authorising the Treasury to loan the Commissioners £30,000 to finance it.

Right: The Commissioners immediately contracted Robert Stevenson to build a new light. To house it he built the baronial style tower, which still dominates the island scene to this day. The lantern room which crowns the structure is 240ft above sea level and originally its light was oil-fired, with fuel refined specially by the Scottish shale oil industry. The stones required for this impressive new lighthouse were prepared for assembly by masons working in the Bell Rock construction yard on the shore at Arbroath and then shipped out to the island. The work of building the new lighthouse took less than two years and, on 1 September

1816, the old coal-fired beacon was finally extinguished and the new light switched on for the first time. Situated on the northeast side of the island its light was described as, 'A group flashing white, showing four flashes in quick succession every half minute.' Even before it was eventually electrified in the mid-1880s, its original paraffin burning light could be seen from all points of the compass for twenty-one miles around. The May also has a powerful fog horn to give audible warning to approaching vessels. Later a second light, known as the Low Light, was built on the island and came into use in 1843. Using the signals from both lights enables ships to obtain a fix on the island and thus accurately calculate their positions. As well as all of the data on its technical side, the May lighthouse had its domestic side in the days before automation – Stevenson included two houses in his plans. The larger of the two accommodated the principal keeper and his family, while his assistant and again his family had the smaller one. There were also guest apartments so that members of the Commissioners or the staff of Northern Lights could stay on the island. This sometimes happened because weather conditions changed and they could not be safely taken off, but on some occasions during summers in Victorian days some also chose to stay on the May for short holidays. The island has its own underground supply of fresh water from five wells, including one dedicated to St Adrian, but all other supplies had to be ferried out from Granton. For the keepers and their families spells of duty lasted for four weeks before they were relieved. They were then ferried back to Granton where they enjoyed a month ashore at the lighthouse keepers' cottages.

The Northern Lighthouse Board's tender, *Pharos*, still calls at the island, but not so regularly. The present *Pharos*, which was launched by Ferguson's of Port Glasgow on 11 December 1992, is the latest in a long and proud line of no fewer than ten lighthouse tenders to bear this very appropriate name. Her immediate predecessor, also called the *Pharos* (built in 1955), is still in service, but sailing thousands of miles away in very different waters. Renamed *Amazing Grace*, which seems an appropriate name for a Scottish-built ship, she is now operated by Windjammer Barefoot Cruises and is based in Nassau in the Bahamas.

When the new baronial style lighthouse was completed on the May in 1816, its designer, Stevenson, was persuaded by Sir Walter Scott not to demolish the original beacon tower, 'but to ruin it *a la picturesque*', which is what was done. It can still be seen as an object of interest to this day and as the oldest light of its kind in Great Britain. As well as building the new lighthouse tower, Stevenson also built two houses for the chief lighthouse keeper and his family and for the assistant keeper. Prior to 1790 fifteen fishermen and their families lived in the island and during this period it was the custom of the other fishermen of Fife to gather on the island each summer for an annual celebration. Unfortunately the merrymaking ended with the capsizing of one of the visiting fishing boats with the loss of all on board including many of the fishermen's wives and girlfriends.

One early visitor to the May was Ferguson the Scottish poet. He travelled out to the island from Dunbar on a sailing ship called the *Blessed Endeavour*. Today most visitors to the Isle of May come aboard the *May Princess*, sailing daily throughout the summer season, to see its vast flocks of seabirds and as they disembark each boatload is met by one of the wardens of Scottish Natural Heritage, who briefs them on what to see and where it is safe and unsafe to venture. The wardens are also available to answer questions and there are also orientation boards at both landing places.

Right: Sail gives way to steam on the Forth according to this picturesque postcard view of traffic on the river well over a century ago in Victorian times. Sadly the postcard provides no further information about the sailing vessel and the little steam tug, which have none the less been so charmingly preserved for eternity.

When their Lords of the Admiralty set to sea, they travelled in style as shown by this picture postcard photograph of the Admiralty Yacht *Enchantress*, seen here at anchor below the cantilever spans of the Forth Railway Bridge at Queensferry. Their Lordships may well have come north to the Forth on a fact-finding mission to gather information upon which to base their decision as to whether to site Scotland's only Royal Naval Dockyard on the Fife shore at Rosyth.

Above: Another of the graceful yachts built by Ramage & Ferguson at their yard in Leith.

Left: The last vessel which Ramage & Ferguson launched at Leith at the start of the 1930s was the auxiliary barquentine *Mercator*, which it built as a training ship for the Belgian government. She is now berthed as a visitor attraction in the port of Ostend as shown in this postcard picture.

The *Mercator* is rigged as a three-masted schooner, with square sails at the foremast, and is fitted with a Burmeister & Wain diesel engine. There is accomodation on board for about seventy cadets and ten officers, cooks and stewards. On her sea trials she reached a speed of ten knots under power and proved to be a fast sailer and easily handled. (information by W.T. Johnston)

A picture postcard view by R.P. Phillimore, a North Berwick artist, showing Inchkeith during the First World War, with a Coastal Class airship, destroyer, motor boat and B-Class submarine.

Next page: Two wonders of Scottish engineering; the Forth Rail Bridge and RMS *Queen Elizabeth 2* on her 2001 visit to Edinburgh en route to the Norwegian Fiords.